C0-AYJ-403

— A MAVERICK PUBLICATION —

The All Natural Salad Book

by Darcy Williamson

Maverick Publications
Drawer 5007 • Bend, Oregon 97701

Cover photo by John Allgair

*Special thanks to Eve Allgair
for her contributions*

TABLE OF CONTENTS

Introduction

Let me tell you about a salad I was served recently. It was made with orange-flavored gelatin, miniature marshmallows, orange sherbet and canned fruit cocktail. The shimmering salad made a beautiful contrast against the bed of greens on which it was served. The snow white topping (from an aerosol can) decoratively squirted on top, complimented the whole affair.

I ate it out of politeness. All right, I confess. I ate it out of latent glutinous tendencies, though the only thing natural about the salad was the lettuce on which it sat. As I forked the last bite of lettuce to my mouth, I realized that I was the only person at the table who had chosen to eat the garnish. Had I been a "natural food purist," the garnish would have been the only part of the salad I would have consumed.

I am certain most of us have been guilty of preparing, serving and consuming salads as described above. However, with our present knowledge of the importance of natural foods, it seems foolish to continue to do so. The "weaning" process may not be easy; old habits are hard to break, especially mine. (In grade school I made my threes backwards. That problem wasn't corrected overnight, either.) I found, as I am certain you will, the results well worth the effort. As a side or main dish, a natural salad can be a taste tempting, nutritional and esthetically pleasant addition to any menu.

Salads and Nutrition

What is a "natural salad"? That's a good question, and one not easily answered. The meaning of "natural" varies from person to person. The only way that I am able to answer that question is by emphasizing what natural means to me: No additives. No chemicals. No refined sugars. No canned or bottled ingredients. No denuded grains. No animal flesh.

Therefore, the recipes in this book exclude the above mentioned.

Now that that's straightened out, here's a brief run-down on vitamins and minerals found in ingredients used in natural salads, followed by a partial list of foods high in the particular vitamin or mineral.

Vitamin A is not only important for growth and repair, it also protects our bodies against infection, keeps our skin healthy and helps our vision. Vitamin A is a fat-soluble vitamin which is stored in the liver.

Spinach	*Asparagus*	*Carrots*
Alfalfa	*Apricots*	*Cantaloupe*
Broccoli	*Peaches*	*Tomatoes*
Egg Yolk	*Natural Cheese*	*Melon*
Squash	*Yams*	*Whole Milk*
Lettuce	*Watercress*	*Apples*

Vitamin B Complex is made up of a large number of separate vitamins. Vitamin B dissolves in water and, therefore, is not easily stored. Our daily diet must include an adequate amount of Vitamin B. Vitamin B has a positive effect upon our nerves, heart, digestion, tissues, skin and mental attitude. Foods containing Vitamin B should be eaten fresh. If you feel that cooking foods rich in Vitamin B is necessary, steam them briefly with a small amount of water.

Green Peas	Spinach	Brown Rice
Soybeans	Lettuce	Potatoes
Butter	Whole Milk	Yogurt
Rye	Tofu	Wheat
Pumpkin Seeds	Beets	Sunflower Seeds
Almonds	Raw Cashews	Pecans
Brewer's Yeast	Beans	Wheat Bran
Peanuts	Oats	Bananas
Avocado	Walnuts	Green Peppers
Carrots	Molasses	

Biotin helps promote healthy hair and stimulates its growth. Next time your hair starts falling out, drink a large glass of freshly squeezed orange juice to which you've added 1 Tbsp. of brewer's yeast. Repeat treatment several times daily.

Brewer's Yeast	Unpolished Rice	Soybeans

Folic Acid helps prevent premature greying of the hair (not its most important function, but I got your attention, didn't I?). Folic acid is essential for the formation of red blood cells, the production of RNA and DNA, combating infections and promoting beautiful skin and hair.

Broccoli	Asparagus	Lima Beans
Irish Potatoes	Spinach	Lettuce
Brewer's Yeast	Wheat Germ	Mushrooms
Raw Cashews	Walnuts	Pecans
Peanuts	Endive	Watercress

PABA stimulates growth when you're young and prevents skin changes due later on in life.

Brewer's Yeast	Brown Rice	Whole Milk
Wheat	Eggs	Yogurt
Wheat Germ	Molasses	Rye
Barley	Triticale	

Pantothenic Acid is involved in all vital functions of the body. It increases vitality and protects us against many physical and mental stresses. Pantothenic acid also helps us ward off infections. As if it doesn't do enough all ready, Pantothenic acid helps prevent premature wrinkles and other signs of aging.

Brewer's Yeast	Wheat Germ	Wheat Bran
Peas	Beans	Green Peppers
Natural Honey	Wheat	Rye
Cucumbers	Peanuts	Egg Yolk
Unsulfured Molasses	Whole Grain Breads	Broccoli
Zucchini	Lettuce	Whole Grain Cereals

Vitamin C is necessary for the tissues of our bodies. As with Vitamin B, Vitamin C is water-soluble and therefore must be included in our daily diet. Vitamin C assists in the healing of wounds and helps our bodies fight unwanted germs.

Oranges	Grapefruit	Strawberries
Cantaloupe	Green Peppers	Potatoes
Tomatoes	Cucumbers	Broccoli
Cabbage	Yogurt	Tofu
Rose Hips	Lemons	Currants
Apples	Persimmon	Persimmon

Vitamin D helps our bodies use the minerals calcium and phosphorus to build strong bones and teeth (sounds like a milk commercial, doesn't it?) You can stand around in the sun and let the sun's rays change some of the oils in your skin into Vitamin D. You can also get cancer and wrinkles from standing around in the sun too much. It might be a better idea to stand around in the fog once in a while, munching a handful of mushrooms.

Mushrooms	Egg Yolks	Natural Cheese
Whole Milk	Butter	Sprouted Seeds
Pumpkin Seeds	Sunflower Seeds	Sunflower Seeds

Vitamin E is important in maintaining a healthy heart and blood vessels. I probably don't have to remind you that it's terrific for the reproduction system. Vitamin E prevents unsaturated fatty acids, sex hormones and fat soluble vitamins from being destroyed in the body by oxygen.

Whole Wheat	Cold-pressed Vegetable Oils	Soybean Oil
Wheat Germ Oil	Whole Raw Seeds	Whole Grains

Sprouted Seeds	Eggs	Lettuce
Fresh Wheat Germ	Spinach	Watercress
Endive		

Bioflavonoids (sounds like something from a science fiction movie) stengthens capillary walls, therefore, helping to prevent capillary hemorrhaging. It also acts as an anticoagulant.

Oranges	Apples	Bananas
Papaya	Pineapple	Grapes
Lemons	Grapefruit	Buckwheat
Green Peppers	Apricots	Peaches
Strawberries	Currants	Cherries
Prunes	Cucumbers	Green Onions

Vitamin F is important in lowering blood cholesterol and is essential for normal glandular activity. It is also a growth promoting factor.

Soybean Oil	Safflower Oil	Corn Oil
Flaxseed Oil	Unprocessed Vegetable Oils	Sunflower Oil

Vitamin K is especially important for blood coagulation, although it's also known for "building better nails." Vitamin K is also important for normal liver function.

Gelatin	Kelp	Alfalfa
Green Peppers	Soybean Oil	Egg Yolks
Raw Cow's Milk	Endive	Chicory

Calcium, as most of us know, is great for bones and teeth. I didn't realize until recently that calcium is also soothing to the nervous system and helps regulate heart beats.

Yogurt	Tofu	Endive
Chicory	Spinach	Watercress
Cabbage	Brussels Sprouts	Oats
Sesame Seeds	Broccoli	Almonds
Natural Cheese	Whole Milk	Sunflower Seeds
Walnuts	Millet	Lettuce
Navy Beans	Most Raw Vegetables	Dandelion Greens

Phosphorus is an important mineral since calcium is best used when Phosphorus and Vitamin D are present. Phosphorus is widely distributed among our foods and we would have to work hard at getting too little of it. However, for peace of mind, here are a few of the foods containing phosphorus.

Wheat	*Rice*	*Barley*
Corn	*Raisins*	*Walnuts*
Dried Apricots	*Almonds*	*Navy Beans*
Dried Prunes	*Sesame Seeds*	*Dried Peas*
Raw Cashews	*Sunflower Seeds*	*Pumpkin Seeds*
White Beans	*Lentils*	*Egg Yolks*
Tofu	*Yogurt*	*Milk*
Natural Cheese	*Butter*	*Lettuce*
Spinach	*Endive*	*Endive*

Sodium, combined with potassium and chlorine, helps keep our body fluids at a normal level. It is also necessary for hydrochloric acid production in the stomach. With our modern day diet, it is most likely we consume too much sodium (salt). There is plenty of sodium in the foods we eat, yet the majority of us have obtained the habit of reaching for the salt shaker. I could give you a long lecture on the nasty side effects of too much salt, but if you want more information (and nightmares) obtain a copy of *Killer Salt* at your local natural food store.

Beets	*Romaine Lettuce*	*Celery*
Watermelon	*Asparagus*	*Kelp*

Chlorine helps the liver in its detoxifying act. Chlorine also aids in digestion. Webster's describes chlorine as "An element isolated as a heavy greenish-yellow, irritating gas of disagreeable, suffocating odor." That should tell you something. According to Earl Mindell's *Vitamin Bible*, over 15 g. can cause unpleasant side effects. So be certain to keep your mouth closed when you dive into a chlorinated pool.

Watercress	*Avocado*	*Chard*
Tomatoes	*Cabbage*	*Endive*
Kale	*Turnip*	*Celery*
Cucumber	*Pineapple*	*Oats*

Magnesium helps in the utilization of Vitamins B and E, calcium, fats and several trace minerals. It is needed for healthy muscle tone and healthy bones. It is also essential for heart health. Magnesium prevents cholesterol build-up, thus acting as a preventative for atherosclerosis.

Nuts	Soybeans	Kale
Chard	Leafy Green Vegetables	Celery
Beet greens	Alfalfa	Figs
Apples	Lemons	Peaches
Almonds	Whole Grains	Sunflower Seeds
Brown Rice	Sesame Seeds	

Iron builds up the quality of the blood. It is essential for the formation of hemoglobin. Iron aids growth, helps prevent fatigue and promotes resistance to disease.

Egg Yolks	Nuts	Beans
Asparagus	Molasses	Oats
Apricots	Bananas	Prunes
Raisins	Turnips	Beets
Beet Greens	Sunflower Seeds	Sesame Seeds

Copper is required to convert the body's iron into hemoglobin. It is also essential for the utilization of vitamin C. Copper is involved in our healing processes and in keeping our hair color natural.

Peas	Almonds	Prunes
Whole Wheat	Pomegranates	Raisins

Iodine regulates the rate of our metabolism, energy production and body weight. It also regulates much of our physical and mental activity. Iodine is also essential for the health of our thyroid glands.

Swiss Chard	Turnip Greens	Garlic
Watercress	Pineapples	Pears
Artichokes	Citrus Fruits	Egg Yolks
Spinach		

Manganese helps to nourish the nerves and brain and assists in the proper co-ordinative action between brain, nerves and muscles. If you doubt your own such co-ordinative action, prepare a concoction of pureed Brussels sprouts, blueberries, bran kelp and raw egg yolks. If you can drink this mess with a straight face, you've proven you have well nourished nerves, but you may need a little guidance in the brain department.

Spinach	Green Leafy Vegetables	Beets
Grapefruit	Apricots	Bran
Oranges	Brussels Sprouts	Blueberries
Peas	Fresh Wheat Germ	Kelp

Zinc is needed for the proper metabolism of vitamin A. It helps the body to get rid of carbon dioxide. Zinc increases the rate of healing of burns and wounds. I've saved the best part for last. Zinc is essential for normal growth and development of sex organs and for the normal function of the prostate gland.

Wheat Bran	Fresh Wheat Germ	Pumpkin Seeds
Sunflower Seeds	Milk	Brewer's Yeast
Eggs	Onions	Nuts
Leafy Green Vegetables		Sprouted Seeds

If you would like to learn more about vitamins and minerals and their importance in our diet, information can be obtained from the following books:

Are You Confused?, Paavo Airola, 1972; The Complete Home Guide to All the Vitamins, Ruth Adams, 1972; Earl Mindell's Vitamin Bible, Earl Mindell, 1979; How to Get Well, Paavo Airola, 1975; Human Nutrition, Benjamin Burton, 1976; Know Your Nutrition, Linda Clark, 1976; Minerals: Kill or Cure, Ruth Adams, 1976; Vitamins: What They Are and How They Can Benefit You, Henry Borsack, 1971; Which Vitamins Do We Need, Martin Ebon, 1974.

Chapter 1

Tossed Salads

To clean firm lettuce, such as Iceberg, hold the head in both hands and rap the stem end sharply on the counter top or on a heavy cutting board. The core can then be easily removed. Allow cold water to run into the hole from which the core was removed. Turn the head right side up on the drain board. When the lettuce head has drained, remove any wilted leaves. Then pull the head apart. Place the lettuce chunks on a paper or absorbent towel lining the bottom of the vegetable tray or crisper of your refrigerator and chill to crisp.

Romaine lettuce, escarole and other lettuce with firm or rigid leaves should be pulled apart, washed, patted dry and crisped in the refrigerator.

Soft lettuce, such as Boston, Bibb or garden lettuce should first be floated in cold water, then spread on a clean absorbent towel to dry in the air.

A French salad basket is an excellent instrument to use when cleaning lettuce. Fill the basket with greens, hang it on the faucet and let cold water run through the greens. Whirl the basket to remove excess moisture. Allow the greens to remain in the basket as they crisp in the refrigerator.

Remember, the best greens are those which are very green, as they contain more chlorophyl, vitamins and minerals.

When preparing greens for a tossed salad, always tear them into bite-size pieces with your fingers. Never cut the lettuce with a knife. I have heard several reasons for not cutting lettuce which include: 1) A knife leaves a metalic taste on the delicately flavored greens. 2) A knife tends to bruise the tender greens. 3) Only torn lettuce coats itself completely when turned in the dressing. My personal reasons for tearing lettuce, as opposed to cutting, is that it's quicker and torn lettuce has a more attractive natural appearance than that which has been cut.

Salads are best served in glass, pottery or wooden bowls. I prefer eating salads from wooden bowls, but such bowls do take special care. They should never be submerged in soapy dish water, or your next salad may taste of dish washing liquid. Wooden bowls should be

9

wiped clean with a moistened towel, then lightly rubbed with a small amount of olive oil. Once every couple of weeks, the wooden bowl should be wiped with a damp cloth which has been dipped in a solution of baking soda and water, rinsed and set in the sun to dry. Should the bowl pick up the odor of garlic, wipe the bowl clean with a cloth dipped in cider vinegar.

Speaking of garlic, a garlic press beats any other method I've tried for crushing garlic. It's a little harder to clean than a hammer (which crushes garlic quite effectively).

Before you rush to the kitchen to begin throwing together a salad, let me remind you that chemical pesticides can ruin a good thing. Know the source of your produce.

Chicory-Avocado Salad (6 servings)

2 heads chicory, broken into bite-size peices
3 avocado, diced
1/2 cup chopped fresh dill
1/2 tsp. vegetable salt
2 Tbsp. cider vinegar
Dash cayenne
2 cloves garlic, crushed
1 tsp. freshly squeezed lemon juice
1 raw egg yolk
1/4 tsp. honey

Combine chicory, avocado and dill. Mix together remaining ingredients in jar and shake well. Pour over salad and serve at once.

Dandelion Salad with Guacamole Dressing (6 servings)

3 cups tender young dandelion greens
8 radishes, sliced
1 cup watercress, torn
3 cups Iceberg lettuce, torn
2 ripe avodaco
1 clove garlic, crushed
1 Tbsp. lemon juice
1/4 tsp. vegetable salt
3 Tbsp. grated onion
1/4 cup yogurt

Tear greens into small pieces. Add radishes, watercress and lettuce.
Place remaining ingredients in blender container and blend well. Pour over greens just before serving.

Dandelion-Watercress Salad (4 servings)

> 2 cups torn leaf lettuce
> 1 cup young dandelion greens
> 1 cup watercress
> 1 cup sorrel
> 1/4 cup chopped green onion
> 1/2 cup diced green pepper
> **Dressing**

Combine all ingredients except lettuce. Chill. Toss mixture with lettuce just before serving. Pass the dressing.

Endive-Chicory Salad (6 servings)

> 4 heads Belgian endive
> 2 heads chicory
> 1/4 cup minced chives
> 1/4 cup minced parsley
> 1/4 cup grated natural cheddar cheese
> 1/2 cup dressing

Wash and dry greens. Tear endive and chicory into bite-size pieces. Toss greens with chives, parsley and cheese. Add just enough dressing to coat greens. Serve at once.

Endive-Walnut Salad (2 servings)

> 2 heads Belgian endive, quartered lengthwise
> 1/2 cup coarsely chopped walnuts (black walnuts are super!)
> 2 Tbsp. olive oil
> 1 Tbsp. freshly squeezed lemon juice
> Sea salt and pepper to taste

Divide endive between 2 salad plates. Sprinkle with walnuts. Beat together oil and lemon juice. Season with sea salt and pepper. Drizzle dressing over endive.

Field Salad (6 servings)

2 avocado, peeled and sliced
2 cups fresh spinach, torn
2 cups watercress, torn
1/2 cup piñyon nuts
Dressing

Combine avocado, spinach, watercress and piñyon nuts. Serve with dressing of choice.

Four Shades of Green (6 servings)

1 clove garlic
1/2 cup dressing
1 head loose leaf lettuce
2 cups torn spinach leaves
1 bunch watercress, torn
1/2 head Romaine, torn

Rub salad bowl with garlic. Add greens to bowl and toss to mix. Just before serving, add desired dressing.

Green Salad Bowl (8 servings)

1 head Romaine lettuce
10 oz. spinach, torn into bite-size pieces
1/2 cup olive oil
1/4 cup cider vinegar
1/4 tsp. vegetable salt
1/2 tsp. honey
1 tsp. dry mustard
1 tsp. fresh basil
1/2 lb. seedless green grapes

Combine oil, vinegar, salt, honey, mustard and basil. Mix well. Chill.
Line salad bowl with lettuce. Place spinach in center. Surround with grapes. Drizzle with dressing just before serving.

Iceberg Salad (6 servings)

> 6 cups Iceberg lettuce, torn into bite-size pieces
> 3 cups torn spinach
> ½ cup chopped green pepper
> 1 cup sliced raw mushrooms
> Oil and Herb Dressing (page 95)

Toss together lettuce, spinach, green pepper and mushrooms. Chill.

Toss salad with desired amount of dressing just prior to serving.

Mexicali Salad (6 servings)

> 1 head Iceberg lettuce
> 2 avocado, peeled and sliced
> 4 ripe tomatoes, diced
> 3 green onion, chopped
> 1 green pepper chopped
> ½ cup safflower oil
> 1½ tsp. chili powder
> ¼ tsp. vegetable salt
> ¼ cup cider vinegar

Line salad bowl with lettuce leaves and avocado slices. Place tomatoes in center. Top with green pepper and onions.

Combine remaining ingredients and pour over salad just before serving.

Romaine-Iceberg Salad (serves 6)

> 3 cups torn Romaine
> 3 cups torn Iceberg lettuce
> 12 radishes, sliced
> 2 cucumbers, sliced
> 8 green onions, sliced
> Garlic Italian Dressing (page 89)

Toss together Romaine, Iceberg, radishes, cucumbers and green onions.

Just before serving, toss salad with desired amount of dressing.

Seven Greens Salad (8 servings)

1 cup Iceberg lettuce
1 cup chicory
1 cup escarole
1½ cups Romaine lettuce
1 cup watercress
1 cup young dandelion greens
1 cup shredded cabbage
½ tsp. vegetable salt
1 cup dressing

Tear greens into bite-size pieces. Combine all ingredients (except dressing) and toss to mix. Add dressing just before serving.

Special Sprout Salad (serves 2)

2 cups mung bean sprouts
2 cups alfalfa sprouts
1 cup radish sprouts
1 medium avocado, diced
1 cup grated carrot
1½ cups cubed natural Cheddar cheese
¼ cup broken pumpkin seeds
½ cup cucumber, thinly sliced
Dressing

Combine all ingredients, except dressing. Toss well. Chill. Add choice of dressing just before serving.

Spinach-Cucumber Salad (4 servings)

8 cups torn spinach
1 medium cucumber, thinly sliced
1 cup dry roasted peanuts
⅓ cup Fresh Mint Dressing (page 89)

Chill spinach. Marinate cucumber slices in dressing 1 hour. Just before servings, toss spinach with cucumber and peanuts.

Spinach Salad (4 servings)

>   *1 lb. spinach*
>   *¾ tsp. sea salt*
>   *¾ Tbsp. honey*
>   *¾ tsp. paprika*
>   *½ tsp. dry mustard*
>   *1 tsp. Tamari soy sauce*
>   *2 Tbsp. freshly squeezed lemon juice*
>   *¼ cup ripe tomato puree*
>   *¾ cup safflower oil*
>   *2 Tbsp. cider vinegar*

Wash spinach several times to remove all sand and grit. Discard hard stems. Tear spinach into small strips, dry and chill.

Mix together salt, honey, paprika, mustard, soy sauce, lemon juice and puree. Slowly add oil and vinegar alternately while beating with an electric hand mixer. Chill dressing. Add dressing to salad just before serving.

Spinach and Tomato Salad (4 servings)

>   *3 cups fresh spinach, torn*
>   *4 ripe tomatoes, chopped*
>   *4 green onions, sliced*
>   *½ cup Avocado Mayonnaise* (page 83) *or*
>   *Guacamolé Dressing* (page 90)

Combine spinach, tomatoes and onions. Toss with dressing just prior to serving.

Spinach-Yogurt Salad (4 servings)

1 lb. spinach, torn in bite-size pieces
2/3 cup minced onion
1 Tbsp. olive oil
2 cups yogurt
1/2 tsp. sea salt
1/4 tsp. pepper
2 cloves garlic, crushed
2 tsp. fresh mint
2 Tbsp. chopped raw cashews

Combine spinach with onion. Heat oil in skillet. Add spinach-onion mixture and cook until spinach wilts. Remove from heat and cool. Add yogurt, salt, pepper and garlic, top with mint and cashews.

Tossed Greens and Beets (4 servings)

3 cups torn mixed greens
1 1/2 cups cooked beets, cut in julienne strips
1 Spanish onion, sliced and separated into rings
1/2 cup sunflower oil
1/3 cup Lemony French Dressing (page 93)

Combine all ingredients, except dressing. Chill. Toss with dressing just before serving.

Tossed Greens and Raw Mushroom Salad
(serves 6)

> *1 head Romaine lettuce*
> *2 heads leaf lettuce*
> *1/2 lb. mushrooms, thinly sliced*
> *1/2 cup Lemony French Dressing* (page 93)

Wash and dry greens. Tear greens into bite-size pieces. Add mushrooms and toss. Pour dressing over greens and mushrooms just prior to serving. Toss well.

Tossed Summer Salad (serves 4)

> *1 cup asparagus tips, cooked tender crisp*
> *1/2 cup sliced radishes*
> *1/2 cup sliced cucumber*
> *1 cup torn lettuce*
> *1/4 cup minced green pepper*
> *2 Tbsp. minced parsley*
> *4 green onions, minced*
> *1/4 cup grated natural Cheddar cheese*
> *1/4 cup dressing*

Toss all ingredients lightly and serve at once.

Watercress-Endive Salad (6 servings)

> *2 cups watercress, torn*
> *4 heads endive, torn*
> *2 cups cooked beets, cut in julienne strips*
> *1/2 cup pecans*
> *1/2 cup cubed tofu*
> *1/2 to 3/4 cup dressing*

Mix all ingredients (except dressing) in salad bowl. Chill. Toss with desired dressing just before serving.

Watercress-Mushroom Salad (serves 4)

2 cups watercress, torn
2 cups sliced mushrooms
1/2 cup sliced radishes
1/3 cup Basic French Dressing (page 84)

Toss watercress with mushrooms and radishes. Add dressing just prior to serving.

Watercress Salad (4 servings)

2 bunches watercress, torn into 2" lengths
3 green onions with tops, chopped
1/4 tsp. pepper
1/2 tsp. sea salt
1 tsp. honey
2 Tbsp. Tamari soy sauce
1 1/2 Tbsp. cider vinegar
1 dried red chili (approx. 1" long), crushed
2 tsp. crushed sesame seeds

Mix together green onions, pepper, salt, honey, soy sauce, vinegar and crushed chili.
Pour over watercress, then sprinkle with sesame seeds. Serve at room temperature.

Wilted Salad (6 servings)

4 cups torn spinach
4 cups torn loose leaf lettuce
1½ tsp. honey
2 Tbsp. water
1 Tbsp. olive oil
½ tsp. vegetable salt
2 tsp. finely chopped dillweed
½ tsp. dry mustard

Toss greens in salad bowl. Combine remaining ingredients in small saucepan and heat to boiling. Pour over greens and toss. Serve at once.

Zucchini Toss (6 servings)

1 head lettuce, torn in bite-size pieces and chilled
head Romaine, torn and chilled
¼ cup olive oil
3 small zucchini, thinly sliced
½ cup sliced radishes
½ cup sliced green onions
½ cup grated natural Swiss cheese
2 Tbsp. cider vinegar
½ tsp. vegetable salt
1 clove garlic, crushed

Toss greens with oil until well coated. Add zucchini, radishes, onions and cheese. Combine vinegar, salt and garlic. Pour over salad and toss. Serve at once.

Tossed Salad Toppers

whole wheat garlic croutons
toasted sesame seeds
alfalfa sprouts
puffed brown rice
sprinkling of poppy seeds
fresh chopped herbs
guacamole
fresh peas
minced green pepper
shredded cucumber
chilled cooked chick peas
sprouted wheat
sliced water chestnuts
shredded purple cabbage
ground peanuts
minced chervil
shredded beets
chopped raw cranberries
chopped hard cooked egg
sunflower seeds
radish sprouts
grated carrot
finely sliced raw mushrooms
roasted soy beans
cubed tofu
shredded raw zucchini
diced jicama

sprouted sunflower seeds
sliced radishes
dash of dill
minced Spanish onion
chopped Jerusalem artichoke
slivered almonds
cauliflowerettes
legume sprouts
grated turnips
broken raw cashews
pumpkin seeds
grated natural cheese
minced chives
chopped watercress
toasted wheat germ
chopped ripe tomato
shelled pinyon nuts
minced celery tops
toasted brown rice
caraway seeds
cooked bulghur
chopped parsley
chopped broccoli
diced avocado
fresh aphids

Chapter 2

Vegetable Salads

Fresh vegetables are at their best when used raw. Certain vegetables; however, (such as artichokes) are unpleasant in their natural state. When cooking is necessary, vegetables should be steamed. A steamer basket, which adjusts to the size of standard saucepans, works well. These metal baskets are inexpensive and can be purchased at natural food stores or gourmet shops. It is important not to over-cook vegetables, for the longer they cook, the less vitamins and minerals they retain.

Vegetable salads appear more interesting when a garnish has been added. The following garnishes are quite popular and easy to prepare:

Celery Curls Use large crisp green stalks. Cut into 2" lengths. Make lengthwise slits, close together, from each end of the stalk, leaving ½" uncut in the center. Soak prepared celery lengths in ice water for 1 hour to make ends curl.

Radish Roses Slice off root and stem ends. Make lengthwise slits around radish, leaving bottom uncut. With point of knife, gently press into open petals. Chill in ice water to make petals unfold.

Fringed Cucumbers Score unpeeled cucumber lengthwise with the tines of a fork; then slice.

Carrot Curls Thinly pare large carrots with vegetable peeler. Fasten curls with toothpick, place in cold water and chill to set curl.

Wilted Vegetables Leave on kitchen countertop for one to two days or until limp and slightly yellowish brown.

Artichoke with Vinaigrette (4 servings)

4 artichokes
1 cup Vinaigrette Dressing (page 99)

Steam artichokes in vegetable steamer 45 minutes or until tender. Chill. Sprinkle chilled artichokes with dressing and pass the remainder when salad is served.

Avocado-Cauliflower Salad (6 servings)

1 medium head cauliflower
Marinade (recipe follows)
1 head Boston lettuce
3 egg yolks, sieved
Watercress
3 avocado, peeled and sliced
3 ripe tomatoes, sliced
1 tsp. freshly squeezed lemon juice

Marinade:
⅔ cup sunflower oil
⅓ cup cider vinegar
2 Tbsp. minced onion
1 clove garlic, crushed
1 tsp. vegetable salt
¾ tsp. dry mustard
1 Tbsp. freshly squeezed lemon juice

Steam whole cauliflower until tender crisp. Divide into sections. Combine marinade ingedients and mix well. Pour over cauliflower and let stand at room temperature 2 hours. Chill.

Place cauliflower on lettuce lined platter. Sprinkle with egg yolk and surround with watercress, avocado and tomatoes. Serve with remaining marinade.

Avocado-Egg Salad (serves 2)

2 cups diced avocado
2 hard-cooked eggs, chopped
3 medium, fully ripened tomatoes, chopped
2 tsp. grated onion
1 tsp. freshly squeezed lemon juice
¼ tsp. sea salt
Dash freshly ground pepper (optional)
½ tsp. honey
¼ cup dressing
Lettuce

Combine avocado, eggs, tomatoes, onion and seasonings. Add desired dressing and toss until well blended. Serve on lettuce.

Avocado-Sprout-Mushroom Salad (4 servings)

2 Tbsp. cider vinegar
2 Tbsp. olive oil
1 Tbsp. safflower oil
¼ tsp. ground cumin
Vegetable salt to taste
2 cups alfalfa sprouts
1 medium avocado, peeled and sliced
¼ lb. mushrooms, sliced

Combine first 5 ingedients and beat vigorously with fork until blended. Arrange sprouts on 4 salad plates; top with avocado and mushrooms. Beat dressing again before adding to salad.

Bean and Tomato Salad (5 to 6 servings)

1 lb. green beans, broken into bite-size pieces
1 tsp. sea salt
2 large tomatoes, quartered
1/2 cup Lemony French Dressing (page 93)

Steam beans until just tender. Sprinkle with a little sea salt. Chill.
Put beans in bowl with quartered tomatoes. Pour dressing over and
toss gently.

Beet Salad with Mint Dressing (4 servings)

2 1/2 cups cooked sliced beets
1/2 cup sliced Bermuda onion
3 Tbsp. safflower oil
3 Tbsp. peanut oil
1/4 cup freshly squeezed orange juice
2 tsp. minced fresh mint

Combine all ingredients. Refrigerate at least 2 hours before serving.

Brussels Sprout and Tomato Salad (4 to 5 servings)

4 cups hot cooked Brussels sprouts
1/2 cup Vinaigrette Dressing (page 99)
1/2 pint cherry tomatoes
6 cups torn spinach

Pour dressing over hot sprouts, tossing to coat each well. Cool.
Refrigerate, covered, 4 hours.
Halve tomatoes, add sprouts and toss. Serve in spinach lined
bowls.

Buffet Vegetable Platter (serves 6 to 8)

1 medium jicama, cut in julienne strips
2 green pepper, cut in rings
2 medium cucumbers, scored and sliced
1 pint cherry tomatoes
¼ lb. small mushrooms
4 medium carrots, scraped and cut into julienne strips
1 bunch green onions, root ends removed and tops trimmed
1 bunch radishes, trimmed
1 bunch loose leaf lettuce, washed and dried

Arrange lettuce attractively on platter. Artistically arrange prepared vegetables. Serve with a variety of dressings. A nice touch is a decrative bowl filled with toasted sesame seeds. The vegetables can then be dipped in seeds after they have been dipped in dressing.

Cabbage and Beet Slaw (6 to 8 servings)

1 head cabbage, shredded
2 large cooked beets, shredded
1 large green pepper, chopped
1 cup Mayonnaise (page 83)
2 Tbsp. cider vinegar
1 Tbsp. honey

Combine cabbage, beets and green pepper. Mix together Mayonnaise, vinegar and honey. Toss dressing with vegetables. Chill.

Carrot and Raisin Salad (4 servings)

4 cups grated carrots
1½ cups raisins
¼ cup sunflower seeds
½ cup Mayonnaise (page 83)
Paprika

Combine carrots, raisins, sunflower seeds and mayonnaise. Mound in bowl and garnish with paprika. Chill.

Celery Root Salad (4 to 5 servings)

1 lb. celery root
½ cup Spicy Italian Dressing (page 99) **or**
    Egg Vinaigrette (page 88)

Scrub celery root. Boil in salted water until tender. Plunge root into ice water. Peel and slice root very thin. Pour dressing over sliced root and allow to marinate 3 to 4 hours.

Celery Victor (8 servings)

8 celery hearts
Vegetable broth
Watercress
1 to 1½ cups Vinaigrette Dressing (page 99)

Cook celery in vegetable broth until celery is tender-crisp. Remove celery from broth and chill. Serve on bed of watercress and spoon desired amount of dressing over celery.

Cole Slaw (6 servings)

½ tsp. vegetable salt
¼ tsp. pepper
½ Tbsp. honey
½ tsp. dry mustard
½ tsp. celery seed
3 Tbsp. freshly squeezed lemon juice
½ cup olive oil
4 cups shredded cabbage (a mixture of green and purple is nice)
1 green pepper, seeded and chopped
2 Tbsp. minced parsley

Blend all seasonings with lemon juice and oil. Add cabbage, green pepper and parsley. Mix well. Chill before serving.

Cooked Cauliflower Salad (5 to 6 servings)

1 large head cauliflower, cooked tender-crisp
Salad greens
2 ripe tomatoes, cut in eighths
1 green pepper, cut in strips
½ cup Mayonnaise (page 83)
1 Tbsp. freshly squeezed lemon juice
2 Tbsp. finely chopped parsley
2 Tbsp. minced chives

Break apart cauliflower. Toss with tomatoes and green pepper. Chill.

Combine mayonnaise with lemon juice. Mix with chilled salad, arrange in bed of salad greens and sprinkle with chives and parsley.

Cucumbers with Curry Dressing (4 servings)

2 cucumbers, thinly sliced
½ tsp. vegetable salt
1 Tbsp. peanut oil
1 Tbsp. sesame oil
1 Tbsp. cider vinegar
1 tsp. honey
2 tsp. curry powder
2 tsp. Tamari soy sauce
2 cloves garlic, crushed

Combine dressing ingredients and pour over cucumbers. Allow to marinate, refrigerated, at least 2 hours.

Cucumber Salad with Raisins (Serves 4)

2 large cucumbers, grated
1½ cups yogurt
¼ cup raisins
¼ cup finely chopped walnuts
1 medium onion, minced
½ tsp. vegetable salt
¼ tsp. pepper
2 tsp. chopped mint

Combine all ingredients. Chill

Eggplant Salad (4 servings)

>   *1 large eggplant, peeled and diced*
>   *Juice of 1 lemon*
>   *2 tsp. sea salt*
>   *1 clove garlic, minced*
>   *¼ cup minced onion*
>   *⅓ cup Fresh Mint Dressing* (page 89)
>   *Romaine lettuce*
>   *1 cup Mayonnaise* (page 83)

Cook eggplant in 1 cup water with lemon juice, salt and garlic for 5 minutes until barely tender. Drain water and place cooled eggplant in bowl. Mix in onion, celery and Mint Dressing. Chill 3 to 5 hours. Serve on Romaine with Mayonnaise on the side.

Filled Avocado Salad (6 servings)

>   *½ cup sunflower seed oil*
>   *¼ cup cider vinegar*
>   *½ tsp. vegetable salt*
>   *¼ tsp. freshly ground pepper*
>   *½ tsp. paprika*
>   *3 green onions, minced*
>   *2 tomatoes, chopped*
>   *1 clove garlic, crushed*
>   *3 medium avocado, halved and pitted*

Mix together first five ingredients. Mix together onion, tomatoes and garlic. Add dressing.

Fill centers of avocado with mixture and serve at once.

Fresh Asparagus Vinaigrette (5 to 6 servings)

2½ lbs. asparagus
Vinaigrette Dressing (page 99)

Steam asparagus tender-crisp. Cool. Marinate asparagus in dressing at least 2 hours.

Fresh Mushroom Salad (2 servings)

1 head loose leaf lettuce
¼ lb. fresh mushrooms
2 tsp. freshly squeezed lemon juice
3 Tbsp. olive oil
1 tsp. honey
Dash salt
Dash coarsely ground pepper (optional)

Line two salad plates with lettuce. Slice mushrooms onto lettuce lined plates. Combine remaining ingredients in cup. Beat with fork. Pour over salad.

Gazpacho Salad (4 servings)

4 tomatoes, peeled and sliced
1 Bermuda onion, thinly sliced
2 stalks celery, thinly sliced
½ cup dry whole wheat bread crumbs
¼ tsp. cumin
¼ tsp. chili powder
½ cup Honey French Dressing (page 91)
1 clove garlic, crushed
Lettuce

Alternate layers of vegetables in glass bowl. Sprinkle with bread crumbs. Chill for at least 1 hour.

Mix together remaining ingredients. Pour dressing over salad and toss at table. Serve on lettuce bed.

Jerusalem Artichoke Salad (serves 2)

7 Jerusalem artichokes, thinly sliced
¼ cup thinly sliced red onion
¼ cup Garlic Italian Dressing (page 89)
Loose leaf lettuce

Toss artichokes with onion and dressing. Serve on bed of lettuce.

Marinated Mushrooms (6 servings)

1 lb. small mushrooms
2 Tbsp. Tamari soy sauce
¼ cup saki (optional)
3 Tbsp. cider vinegar
2 Tbsp. minced onion
1 Tbsp. honey
½ tsp. vegetable salt

Combine soy sauce, saki, vinegar, onion, honey and salt. Bring ingredients to boiling over medium heat. Pour over mushrooms. Cool to room temperature, then refrigerate 2 days, stirring occasionally.

Marinated Vegetable Platter (6 servings)

½ lb. carrot sticks
6 cherry tomatoes, halved
6 hard-cooked eggs, halved
½ cup cauliflowerettes
1 medium onion, sliced
4 cooked artichoke hearts (optional)
2 Tbsp. cider vinegar
Dash sea salt
8 Tbsp. safflower oil
¼ tsp. dry mustard

Combine vinegar, salt, oil and mustard in jar and shake to mix. Place vegetables in bowl and pour dressing over. Chill for 2 to 3 hours. Arrange marinated vegetables on serving platter.

Mixed Raw Vegetable Salad (6 servings)

3 cups small mushrooms
1 cup thinly sliced celery
1 green pepper, cut in strips
1 cup cherry tomatoes
1 carrot, scraped and thinly sliced
⅔ cup olive oil
⅓ cup cider vinegar
1 clove garlic, crushed
1 tsp. fresh tarragon, minced
¼ tsp. vegetable salt

Combine vegetables in bowl. Mix together oil, vinegar, garlic, tarragon and salt. Pour over vegetables. Marinate in covered container 8 to 12 hours.

Mung Bean Sprout Salad (serves 2)

1 cup chopped celery
1 cup grated carrots
½ cup piñyon nuts
1½ Tbsp. sesame seeds
2 cups fresh mung bean sprouts
Honey French Dressing (page 91) *or*
Curry French Dressing (page 87)

Combine ingredients (except dressing). Chill. Toss with desired amount of dressing just before serving.

Mushroom-Celery Salad (5 servings)

¾ lb. small fresh mushrooms, thinly sliced
5 stalks celery, thinly sliced
½ cup olive oil
¼ cup freshly squeezed lemon juice
½ tsp. sea salt
¼ tsp. pepper
Loose leaf lettuce

Combine mushrooms and celery. Blend the remaining ingredients together. Toss gently with salad. Chill. Serve on bed of lettuce.

Mushroom-Tofu-Avocado Salad (4 servings)

⅓ cup olive oil
1 Tbsp. cider vinegar
1 Tbsp. garlic, halved
½ tsp. vegetable salt
Juice of 1 lemon
2 avocado, thinly sliced
½ lb. mushrooms, thinly sliced
1 cup cubed tofu

Layer avocado, mushrooms and tofu in bowl. Combine remaining ingredients and pour over ingredients in bowl. Marinate in refrigerator 1 hour.

Peanut-Carrot Salad (4 servings)

> 1 cup whole wheat bread crumbs
> 2 Tbsp. butter
> 2/3 cup peanuts
> 2 cups shredded carrots
> Soybean or safflower oil
> Vinegar
> Lettuce leaves

Melt butter in skillet. Add crumbs and stir until crumbs are lightly browned. Remove from hear. Add peanuts and mix well. Add carrots. Sprinkle with oil and vinegar. Serve on lettuce leaves.

Potato Salad (Serves 8 to 10)

> 2 lbs. new red potatoes, boiled in jackets
> 6 Tbsp. olive oil
> 6 Tbsp. cider vinegar
> 1/2 cup vegetable broth or bouillon
> 1/2 tsp. vegetable salt
> 1/4 tsp. paprika
> 1/4 cup sliced green onions
> 1 Tbsp. minced parsley

Slice potatoes while still warm. Pour a mixture of oil, vinegar and broth over warm potatoes. Marinate 1 hour.

Combine remaining ingredients and fold into salad. Chill.

Raw Vegetable Platter (serves 8)

2 large bunches of watercress or parsley
½ lb. zucchini, thinly sliced
1 head cauliflower, separated
1 bunch celery, cut in 3" sections
8 green onions, trimmed
6 carrots, cut in strips
1 carton cherry tomatoes
2 green peppers, sliced
2 kohlrabi, thinly sliced
½ cub Horseradish Herb Dressing (page 92) *or*
Herbed Yogurt Dressing (page 91)

Line platter with watercress or parsley. Assemble vegetables attractively on platter. Add dressing just prior to serving.

Sauerkraut Salad (serves 4 to 5)

3 cups sauerkraut
1 cup thinly sliced green onion
1 cup shredded carrots
½ cup minced celery
½ cup minced green pepper
1 tsp. caraway seeds
⅓ cup safflower oil
⅓ cup cider vinegar
2 Tbsp. honey

Rinse sauerkraut, in colander, under running water. Drain. Dump kraut into bowl. Add vegetables and caraway seeds. Mix well.

In small jar, combine remaining ingredients. Shake vigorously. Pour dressing over salad and toss to mix. Serve on bed of fresh greens.

Shredded Cucumber Salad (Serves 4)

2 large cucumbers
1 Tbsp. vegetable salt
1 Tbsp. peanut oil
1 Tbsp. Tamari soy sauce
1 Tbsp. sesame oil
2 cloves garlic, crushed
1/2 tsp. honey
Dash cayenne

Shred unpeeled cucumber and sprinkle with salt. Allow to stand in refrigerator for several hours. Rinse in sieve under cold water. Drain thoroughly and squeeze out any excess moisture.

Combine remaining ingredients and mix well. Pour over cucumbers.

Simple Zucchini Salad (6 servings)

6 small zucchini, sliced and steamed tender-crisp
1/4 cup Herbed Yogurt Dressing (page 91)
Lettuce
Paprika

Combine dressing with chilled zucchini. Toss gently. Serve on a bed of lettuce leaves. Sprinkle with paprika.

Spanish Potato Salad (serves 6)

2 cloves garlic, minced
1 cup whole wheat bread cubes
1 Tbsp. peanut oil
2 cups diced cooked potatoes
2 stalks celery, cut-up
1 medium onion, chopped
1 medium carrot, chopped
½ cup chopped green pepper
¼ cup safflower oil
3 Tbsp. cider vinegar
½ tsp. vegetable oil
1 tsp. chili powder
1 head lettuce, broken in chunks

Saute' garlic and bread cubes in peanut oil until golden. Remove bread crumbs and set aside.

Put potatoes and vegetables in mixing bowl. Combine oil, vinegar, salt and chili powder. Pour over vegetables in bowl and toss gently. Chill at least 1 hour before serving. Just before serving, toss with bread cubes and lettuce.

Tomato and Avocado Salad (4 servings)

2 tomatoes, peeled and cut in wedges
1 avocado, peeled and sliced
⅓ cup Lemony French Dressing (page 93)
½ head lettuce
3 Tbsp. grated natural Cheddar cheese

Marinate tomatoes and avocado in dressing for 1 or 2 hours. Tear lettuce into bite-size pieces into salad bowl. Add tomatoes and avocado, sprinkle with cheese and toss lightly.

Tomato Salad (3 to 4 servings)

2 tomatoes
½ cup olive oil
3 Tbsp. cider vinegar
1 tsp. Tamari soy sauce
½ tsp. vegetable salt
½ clove minced garlic
1 tsp. sweet basil
½ tsp. thyme
2 Tbsp. chopped green onion

Slice tomatoes and place in medium-size bowl. Combine remaining ingredients; pour over tomatoes. Refrigerate 1 hour.

Serve on bed of lettuce.

Turnip-Carrot Salad (4 servings)

4 cups thinly sliced turnips
1 cup thinly sliced carrots
1 Tbsp. vegetable salt
½ cup cider vinegar
1½ Tbsp. honey
½ tsp. grated fresh ginger root

Sprinkle turnips and carrots with salt and let stand for 1 hour. Rinse and press out moisture.

Mix remaining ingredients and pour over salad. Chill.

Zucchini Salad (6 servings)

6 small zucchini, thinly sliced
2 tomatoes, peeled and coarsly chopped
1 green pepper, chopped
1 cup chopped Spanish onion
1 tsp. honey
½ tsp. vegetable salt
¼ tsp. pepper
¼ tsp. paprika
3 Tbsp. Mayonnaise (page 83) *or*
   Spicy Italian Dressing (page 99)

Combine all ingredients and mix well. Serve on bed of greens.

Chapter 3

Molded Salads

Asparagus-Egg Mold (serves 6)

1 lb. asparagus, cut in 1½" pieces
1 envelope unflavored gelatin
2 Tbsp. grated onion
¼ tsp. vegetable salt
1 Tbsp. freshly squeezed lemon juice
1 cup Mayonnaise (page 83)
3 hard-cooked eggs, chopped

Steam asparagus tender-crisp. Add ½ tsp. salt to liquid remaining in saucepan from steamed asparagus; then and enough water to bring liquid to 1 cup. Soften gelatin in ¼ cup cold water for 5 minutes; then add to liquid in saucepan. Stir until gelatin has completely dissolved. Add onion, salt, lemon juice and Mayonnaise. Chill until syrupy. Fold in steamed asparagus and chopped eggs. Pour into 1½ qt. mold and chill until set. Unmold onto lettuce lined plate.

Asparagus Mold (6 servings)

> 2 pkg. unflavored gelatin
> 1/2 cup cold water
> 2 Tbsp. honey
> 2 vegetable bouillon cubes
> 1 1/2 cups boiling water
> 1/2 cup Herbed Yogurt Dressing (page 91)
> 3 Tbsp. freshly squeezed lemon juice
> 2 cups cooked asparagus, cut up
> 1/2 cup diced celery
> 1/4 cup finely chopped green pepper
> Lettuce leaves
> Mayonnaise (page 83), optional

Soften gelatin in cold water. Add honey, bouillon and boiling water, stirring until gelatin has dissolved. Add Herbed Yogurt Dressing and lemon juice, stirring until smooth. Chill until slightly thickened.

Stir asparagus, celery and green pepper into gelatin mixture. Pour into lightly oiled 1 qt. mold and chill until salad is firm.

Unmold on lettuce leaves. Serve with Mayonnaise, if desired.

Asparagus Mousse (6 servings)

> 1 envelope unflavored gelatin
> 1 Tbsp. cider vinegar
> 1 Tbsp. freshly squeezed lemon juice
> 1/2 tsp. vegetable salt
> Dash cayenne
> Dash paprika
> 3 cups diced asparagus, steamed tender-crisp (reserve 1/2 cup liquid)
> 1 Tbsp. minced ripe tomato
> 2 tsp. grated onion

Dissolve gelatin in a little cold water. Heat reserved asparagus liquid and stir into softened gelatin. Add seasonings and chill until syrupy. Fold in asparagus, tomato and onion. Pour into mold and chill.

Avocado-Sunflower Mold (4 servings)

1 envelope unflavored gelatin
1/2 cup hot water
1 Tbsp. freshly squeezed lemon juice
1 cup yogurt
1/2 tsp. vegetable salt
1 thin slice onion
Dash cayenne
1 medium avocado, peeled and pitted
2/3 cup sunflower seeds

Place gelatin and water in blender container and blend at high speed 30 seconds. Add lemon juice, yogurt, salt, onion, cayenne and avocado. Blend at high speed until smooth. Pour into mold and chill until salad begins to set. Stir in seeds and chill until firm. Unmold on platter and serve with additional yogurt, if desired.

Cranberry Mold (6 servings)

2 envelopes unflavored gelatin
1 cup hot apple juice
1/2 cup honey
1 Tbsp. freshly squeezed lemon juice
Juice of 1 orange
1 cup raw cranberries, ground in food grinder
Grated rind of 1 orange
1 Tbsp. grated lemon rind
1/2 cup chopped walnuts
1 cup chopped celery

Soften gelatin in 1/2 cup water. Add hot juice and stir until gelatin has completely dissolved. Add honey, lemon and orange juice. Chill until thickened.

Stir in remaining ingredients and pour into mold. Chill until set.

Cranberry-Pineapple Mold (serves 4)

1 pkg. unflavored gelatin
1/4 cup cold water
1/2 cup boiling water
1/4 cup honey
1/2 tsp. grated lemon rind
2 cups raw cranberries, finely chopped
1 cup unsweetened pineapple juice

Soften gelatin in cold water 5 minutes. Add boiling water and stir to dissolve. Stir in honey and rind. Add cranberries and pineapple juice. Chill until syrupy. Stir, pour into mold and chill until firm.

Cucumber Mold (6 servings)

1 envelope unflavored gelatin
1/4 cup freshly squeezed lime juice
3 Tbsp. honey
1/2 cup carrot juice
1/2 cup boiling water
1 Tbsp. cider vinegar
1 tsp. onion juice
1 large cucumber, peeled and chopped
1/2 cup cubed tofu
1 cup yogurt

Combine gelatin, lime juice, honey and carrot juice in bowl. Stir well. Allow gelatin to soften 10 minutes. Add boiling water to gelatin mixture and stir well. Add vinegar and lemon juice. Stir. Chill until partially set.

Blend yogurt, cucumber and tofu into partially set gelatin. Pour into mold. Chill. Unmold on lettuce lined plate.

Golden Glow Salad (4 to 5 servings)

1 envelope unflavored gelatin
¼ cup cold water
1½ cups freshly squeezed grapefruit juice
2 Tbsp. honey
1½ cups grated carrots
1 cup orange sections
Salad greens

Soften gelatin in cold water. Combine grapefruit juice with honey and heat over medium heat. Stir in softened gelatin. Cool until slightly thickened. Fold in carrots and orange sections. Pour into mold. Chill until firm. Unmold on greens. Serve with dressing, if desired.

Green Pea Mousse Mold (4 servings)

1 envelope unflavored gelatin
¼ cup cold water
¾ cup boiling water
2 cups cooked fresh peas
¼ tsp. vegetable salt
Dash cayenne
1 cup yogurt

Soften gelatin in cold water. Add boiling water and stir until gelatin dissolves.

Puree peas in blender along with salt, cayenne and yogurt. Stir into gelatin. Chill until syrupy; stir, then pour into 4 cup mold and chill until firm.

Herbed Tomato Aspic (serves 4)

¼ cup chopped celery
¼ cup chopped onion
½ tsp. vegetable salt
2 tsp. honey
1 tsp. chopped fresh basil
1 Tbsp. cider vinegar
2 cups tomato juice
2 tsp. chopped fresh oregano
2 Tbsp. gelatin
Mayonnaise (page 83) *optional*

Cook celery and onion with seasonings in tomato juice until celery and onion are tender-crisp. Mix gelatin with ½ cup cold water and add to hot tomato mixture. Stir to dissolve. Pour into mold. Chill. Serve with Mayonnaise, if desired.

Peach Aspic (serves 6)

1 envelope unflavored gelatin
½ cup boiling water
5 ripe peaches, peeled and sliced
1 Tbsp. honey
¼ cup cider vinegar
½ cup fresh tomato puree
3 Tbsp. freshly squeezed lemon juice
¼ tsp. sea salt

Put boiling water and gelatin in blender container. Add remaining ingredients and blend to puree. Pour into loaf pan; chill until firm.

Prune Aspic (serves 6 to 8)

2 envelopes unflavored gelatin
2 cups prune juice, heated
2 cups pitted, coarsely chopped cooked prunes
2 Tbsp. freshly squeezed lemon juice
2 tsp. grated lemon rind

Soften gelatin in ½ cup cool water. Stir in heated prune juice and mix until gelatin has dissolved. Let mixture thicken slightly, then stir in prunes, lemon juice and rind.

Molded Apple Salad (6 servings)

½ cup cold water
2 Tbsp. unflavored gelatin
2 cups unsweetened apple juice
2 medium-size apples, diced
½ cup chopped walnuts
1 Tbsp. snipped parsley

Soften gelatin in water. Stir in hot apple juice and continue stirring until gelatin has dissolved. Cool; chill until slightly thickened. Stir in remaining ingredients and chill until firm. Serve on bed of lettuce.

Molded Beet Salad (serves 4)

2 cups cooked, diced beets
Dash sea salt
1½ Tbsp. honey
½ tsp. grated horseradish
¼ cup cider vinegar
1 envelope unflavored gelatin
1 cup warm beet liquid
1 cup thinly sliced celery
¼ cup chopped green pepper
Lettuce leaves

In bowl combine beets, salt, honey, horseradish and vinegar. In separate bowl, dissolve gelatin in beet liquid. Chill gelatin mixture until almost set. Blend in beet mixture, celery and green pepper. Pour into mold. Chill until set. Unmold on lettuce leaves.

Molded Broccoli Salad (12 servings)

4 eggs, hard-cooked and chopped
3 cups broccoli, cooked tender-crisp and chopped
1 8-oz. pkg. cream cheese, cut in pieces
1½ cups vegetable bouillon
1 envelope unflavored gelatin
1 Tbsp. Tamari soy sauce
3 Tbsp. freshly squeezed lemon juice
1 tsp. vegetable salt
1 tsp. hot pepper sauce, optional

Heat 1 cup bouillon, add cream cheese and stir until cream cheese has melted. Soften gelatin in ½ cup bouillon. Stir into warm bouillon-cream cheese mixture. Add broccoli and remaining ingredients. Chill in lightly oiled rectangular glass pan until firm.

Molded Egg Garden Salad (6 servings)

1 envelope unflavored gelatin
¼ cup cold water
½ cup boiling water
6 hard-cooked eggs, chopped
½ cup sliced green onions
½ cup sliced radishes
½ tsp. dry mustard
½ tsp. Tamari soy sauce
¼ tsp. sea salt
2 Tbsp. cider vinegar
¼ cup water

Soften gelatin in cold water. Add boiling water and stir to dissolve gelatin. Add mustard, soy sauce, salt, vinegar and ¼ cup water. Pour gelatin mixture in bowl and chill until syrupy.

Combine eggs, onions and radishes. Fold into gelatin mixture and chill until set. Unmold on greens, if desired.

Molded Fresh Fruit Salad (8 servings)

2 pkg. unflavored gelatin
1 cup cold water
¾ cup boiling water
⅓ cup honey
½ cup freshly squeezed lime juice
1 cup seedless grapes
1 cup watermelon chunks
1 cup peeled and sliced peaches
1 cup cantaloupe pieces

Sprinkle gelatin over 1 cup water to soften. Add boiling water and stir to dissolve gelatin. Add lime juice. Arrange a small amount of fruit in bottom of mold to form a design. Spoon on just enough gelatin mixture to cover bottom of mold; chill until nearly firm. Chill remaining gelatin mixture until thickened. Fold in remaining fruit. Spoon into mold. Chill until firm. Unmold on platter.

Molded Gaucamole Salad (serves 6)

1/2 cup cold water
2 envelopes unflavored gelatin
1/2 cup boiling water
2 large avocado, peeled and sliced
3 Tbsp. freshly squeezed lemon juice
1 cup yogurt
1/2 tsp. vegetable salt
1 tsp. chili powder
Hot pepper sauce to taste

Soften gelatin in cold water 10 minutes. Add boiling water and stir to dissolve.

Put gelatin, along with remaining ingredients, in blender container and liquefy. Pour into mold and chill until firm.

Molded Pomegranate Salad (6 servings)

Seeds from 6 medium pomegranates
2 1/2 cups water
2 sliced lemon
3/4 cup water
3 Tbsp. unflavored gelatin
2/3 cup honey
Loose leaf lettuce

Set aside 1 cup pomegranate seeds. Place remaining seeds in saucepan with 2 1/2 cups water and lemon. Cover and simmer 15 minutes. Strain juice and discard pulp. Stir in honey. Soften gelatin in 3/4 cup water for 5 minutes. Add hot pomegranate liquid and stir until gelatin has dissolved. Chill until partially set. Add reserved seeds and chill until firm. Serve on bed of lettuce.

Molded Raw Mixed Vegetable Salad (serves 6)

2 envelopes unflavored gelatin
1/4 cup honey
1 tsp. vegetable salt
1 1/2 cups boiling water
1 1/2 cups cold water
1/3 cup cider vinegar
1/4 cup freshly squeezed lemon juice
2 cups shredded cabbage
1 cup thinly sliced celery
1/2 cup tofu, cubed
1 cup shredded carrots

Combine gelatin with honey and salt. Add 1 cup cold water and allow mixture to stand 5 minutes. Add boiling water and stir until gelatin has dissolved. Add remaining cold water, vinegar and lemon juice. Chill until gelatin begins to set. Fold in remaining ingredients. Pour into 9 x 5 x 3" loaf pan. Chill until firm.

Molded Winter Salad (4 to 5 servings)

1 Tbsp. unflavored gelatin
1 cup unsweetened white grape juice
1 1/2 cups alfalfa sprouts
1/2 cup chopped celery
1/2 cup shredded purple cabbage
1/4 cup green pepper
1 apple, seeded and diced

Soften gelatin in 1/4 cup grape juice. Heat remaining juice. Stir into softened gelatin. Cool. Chill until partially set. Mix remaining ingredients into gelatin mixture. Chill until firm. Unmold on bed of greens.

Persimmon Mold (4 servings)

½ cup water
2 Tbsp. unflavored gelatin
2 Tbsp. honey
2 cups hot fresh squeezed grapefruit juice
1½ cups ripe persimmon pulp
2 Tbsp. freshly squeezed lemon juice
Lettuce leaves

Soften gelatin in water. Add honey and hot grapefruit juice and stir until gelatin has dissolved. Chill until mixture has thickened slightly, then add persimmon pulp and lemon juice. Chill until firm. Serve on lettuce leaves.

Tomato Aspic with Sprouts (6 servings)

3½ cups chopped ripe tomatoes
½ tsp. vegetable salt
½ tsp. paprika
1 tsp. honey
2 Tbsp. freshly squeezed lemon juice
3 Tbsp. minced celery (leaves included)
1 tsp. dried basil leaves
2 Tbsp. unflavored gelatin
½ cup cold water
½ cup grated carrots
1 sliced avocado
1 cup alfalfa sprouts
½ cup toasted sesame seeds

Combine tomatoes, salt, paprika, honey, lemon juice, celery and basil in saucepan. Bring to boiling; reduce heat and simmer for 30 minutes. Strain, discarding solids.

Soak gelatin in ½ cup cold water 10 minutes. Stir into hot juice and add water to make 4 cups. Pour into mold or pan. Chill.

When aspic is about to set, stir in remaining ingredients. Chill until set. Unmold on platter. Good topped with a dab of yogurt.

Vegetable Salad Mold (serves 4)

2 cups diced steamed vegetables
1 cup diced celery
1 cup seedless grapes, halved
3 Tbsp. minced parsley
½ tsp. sea salt
1½ Tbsp. unflavored gelatin
½ cup hot vegetable stock
1 cup Mayonnaise (page 83)
2 Tbsp. yogurt
Lettuce or watercress

Mix together vegetables, celery, grapes and parsley. Season with salt.

Soften gelatin in ¼ cup cold water. Add hot stock and stir to dissolve. Stir into vegetable mixture. Chill until slightly thickened. Combine Mayonnaise with yogurt. Fold into vegetable-gelatin mixture. Spoon into mold and chill. Unmold on bed of lettuce or watercress leaves.

Vegetables in Aspic (4 to 5 servings)

1 envelope unflavored gelatin
¾ cup vegetable broth
½ cup tomato juice
10 steamed asparagus tips
1 cup raw peas
Lettuce
¾ cup Mayonnaise (page 83)

Soften gelatin in ¼ cup cold water. Heat broth and pour over gelatin to dissolve. Add juice. Pour some mixture into mold to depth of ¼". Chill. When set, arrange asparagus tips. Chill. Chill remaining gelatin until syrupy; fold in peas and add to mold. Chill until firm. Unmold on lettuce and serve with Mayonnaise.

Yogurt-Waldorf Mold (4 servings)

1 envelope unflavored gelatin
1 cup hot unsweetened apple juice
1 cup yogurt
1 apple, cored and chopped
¼ cup chopped celery
¼ cup chopped walnuts
¼ cup toasted sesame seeds

Dissolve gelatin in hot apple juice. Chill until partially set. Fold in remaining ingredients. Chill until firm.

Chapter 4

Main Meal Salads

Avocado with Cottage Cheese (6 servings)

2 lbs. creamed cottage cheese
2 medium tomatoes, diced
½ cup chopped green pepper
¼ tsp. dill weed
3 avocado, halved and peeled
Loose leaf lettuce
1 cup chopped raw cashews

Combine cottage cheese, tomatoes, green pepper and dill. Arrange avocado halves on lettuce lined salad plates and mound cheese mixture on top. Sprinkle with nuts. Great served with rice crackers and mint iced tea!

Brown Rice and Fresh Fruit Salad (3 to 4 servings)

3 cups cooked brown rice
2 ripe nectarines
⅔ cup chopped raw cashews
2 plums, cut into sixths
2 peaches, sliced
1 pear, sliced
Poppy Seed Dressing (page 97)

Puree nectarines in blender. Stir pureed fruit into rice. Add cashews. Line salad bowl with fruit. Top with rice mixture. Serve with dressing.

Brown Rice and Kidney Bean Salad (serves 2)

6 Tbsp. safflower oil
4 Tbsp. cider vinegar
1½ tsp. dry mustard
2 cloves garlic, crushed
¼ tsp. vegetable salt
Dash cayenne
1 cup cooked brown rice
2 cups cooked kidney beans
½ cup diced onion
2 hard-cooked eggs, riced
½ cup sliced celery
2 cups shredded lettuce

Combine oil, vinegar, mustard, garlic, salt and cayenne. Toss with rice, beans, onion, egg and celery. Allow to stand at room temperature 2 hours before serving. Serve on bed of shredded lettuce.

Brown Rice Salad (2 to 3 servings)

2 cups cooked brown rice
3 ripe tomatoes, chopped
2 green peppers, seeded and cut into strips
½ tsp. vegetable salt
¼ tsp. pepper
2 Tbsp. olive oil
1 Tbsp. cider vinegar
½ tsp. dry mustard
Lettuce

Put rice, tomatoes and green pepper in bowl. Combine remaining ingredients. Mix well. Pour over rice mixture and stir gently. Chill. Serve on lettuce.

Chef's Salad (serves 6)

1 head iceberg lettuce, torn
1/2 head Romaine, torn
1/2 cup sliced radishes
1/3 cup sliced green onions and tops
3 avocado, peeled and sliced
1/2 lb. Swiss cheese, cut in Julienne strips
4 hard-cooked eggs, sliced
1 cup cubed tofu
Dressing of choice

Combine greens, radishes and green onions in large salad bowl. Arrange avocado, cheese, eggs and tofu on top of greens in salad bowl. Just before serving, toss with dressing.

Chick Pea-Tofu Salad (4 servings)

2 cups cooked chick peas (garbanzo)
1/2 lb. tofu, diced
1 medium-size sweet onion, sliced thin
1/2 cup olive oil
1/4 cup freshly squeezed lemon juice
1/2 tsp. vegetable salt
1/4 tsp. pepper (optional)
1/2 tsp. coriander
Salad greens

Combine peas, tofu and onion. Mix the rest of the ingredients, except greens, and pour over pea mixture. Let stand for several hours. Toss. Serve on salad greens.

Curried Brown Rice Salad (6 servings)

1 Tbsp. safflower oil
1 cup raw brown rice
2½ cups water
2 Tbsp. curry powder
2 tsp. cardamon
½ tsp. vegetable salt
2 Tbsp. honey
1 cup raisins
½ cup freshly chopped green onions
½ cup minced celery
1 cup diced fresh pineapple
½ cup grated fresh coconut
½ cup chopped peanuts
½ cup chopped tart apple
½ cup Curry French Dressing (page 87)

In saucepan, lightly brown rice in hot oil. Add water, seasoning and honey. Bring to boiling. Reduce heat; cover saucepan. Allow mixture to simmer gently until moisture has been absorbed (approximately 55 minutes). Cool. Chill.

Combine chilled rice with remaining ingredients. Serve on bed of fresh greens.

Dilled Brown Rice Salad (4 servings)

2½ cups chilled cooked brown rice
2 Tbsp. freshly squeezed lemon juice
½ tsp. vegetable salt
1 Tbsp. chopped fresh dill weed
1 ripe tomato, chopped
1 avocado, peeled and diced
½ cup Cottage Cheese-Yogurt Dressing (page 86)

Combine all ingredients and toss gently. Chill before serving.

Fruited Bulgar Salad (3 to 4 servings)

1 cup bulgar wheat
Boiling water
1 cup finely chopped celery
1 cup finely chopped apples
½ cup chopped dates
½ cup chopped dried apricots
½ cup broken walnuts
⅓ cup Yogurt-Lime Dressing (page 100)

Place cracked wheat in oven proof bowl and pour boiling water over to cover. Let stand 2½ to 3 hours. Drain well.

Combine wheat with remaining ingredients. Toss gently. Chill before serving.

Fruit-Cottage Cheese Platter (4 to 5 servings)

Leaf lettuce
2 cups cottage cheese
4 2" wedges cantaloupe
1 pint strawberries, cleaned and hulled
1 cup blueberries
2 cups seedless grapes
2 cups apricot halves
Ginger-Yogurt Dressing (page 89)

Line platter with lettuce. Spoon cottage cheese in center. Arrange melon, strawberries, blueberries, grapes and apricots in groups around cottage cheese. Serve dressing on the side.

Garden Rice Salad (5 to 6 servings)

1 Tbsp. safflower oil
1 cup raw brown rice
2½ cups vegetable stock
1½ Tbsp. curry powder
2 tsp. cardamon
½ tsp. vegetable salt
1 cup finely chopped celery
½ cup minced onion
½ cup finely chopped green pepper
½ cup grated carrots
½ cup thinly sliced radishes
⅔ cup Curry Yogurt Dressing (page 88)

In saucepen, lightly brown rice in hot oil. Add to rice, vegetable stock, curry, cardamon and salt and bring to boiling. Reduce heat, cover saucepan and allow mixture to simmer gently 55 minutes or until all moisture has been absorbed. Cool. Chill.

Add remaining ingredients, mix well and refrigerate until served.

Macaroni and Cheese Salad (4 servings)

2 cups cooked macaroni (whole wheat or soy)
2 Tbsp. chopped green onion
2 Tbsp. chopped ripe tomato
2 Tbsp. chopped green pepper
½ cup diced celery
1 cup shredded natural Cheddar cheese
½ tsp. sea salt
Dash cayenne
¾ cup Caraway Mayonnaise (page 85)
Lettuce

Combine macaroni, onion, tomato, green pepper, celery and cheese. Season Caraway Mayonnaise with salt and cayenne. Add dressing to salad and toss. Chill. Serve on platter lined with crisp lettuce.

Macaroni Supper Salad (5 to 6 servings)

8 oz. whole wheat or green elbow macaroni
1 cup Mayonnaise (page 83)
1/4 cup safflower oil
1/4 cup cider vinegar
1 tsp. dry mustard
1/2 tsp. vegetable salt
1 clove garlic, crushed
1 tsp. fresh oregano
2 cups thinly sliced cucumber
1 1/2 cups diced ripe tomato
1/2 cup diced green pepper
1/4 cup minced green onion
Dash cayenne
2 cups diced natural Swiss cheese
2 hard-cooked eggs, chopped
Lettuce leaves
Chopped parsley

Cook macaroni. Drain; rinse with cold water.

In bowl, combine Mayonnaise, oil, vinegar, mustard, salt, garlic and oregano. Mix well. Add vegetables, cheese and macaroni; toss to mix well. Chill, covered.

Just before serving, toss with chopped eggs. Spoon into lettuce lined serving bowl. Garnish with parsley.

Mushroom-Swiss Salad (4 servings)

1 1/2 cup thinly sliced mushrooms
1/2 cup julienned carrots
1/2 cup juilienned celery
1/2 cup thinly sliced Natural Swiss cheese
1/4 cup olive oil
3 Tbsp. freshly squeezed lemon juice
1/2 tsp. sea salt
1/4 tsp. pepper

Combine mushrooms, carrots, celery and Swiss. Mix remaining ingredients and pour over vegetables. Toss gently. Chill.

Pasta Salad (4 servings)

8 oz. whole wheat macaroni, cooked, rinsed and chilled
½ cup olive oil
⅓ cup cider vinegar
2 Tbsp. chopped fresh basil
1 clove garlic, crushed
⅔ cup grated natural Jack cheese
½ tsp. vegetable salt
Dash cayenne
¼ cup minced parsley
1 red pepper, minced

Combine chilled macaroni with remaining ingredients. Toss well. Serve on bed of fresh greens.

Pilaf Filled Tomatoes (6 servings)

1 cup bulgar
1 cup vegetable broth
3 Tbsp. chopped parsley
¼ cup grated carrot
½ cup thinly sliced green onion
2 cups natural Cheddar cheese
1 cup fresh corn (cut off cob)
6 large tomatoes
Lettuce

Combine bulgar and broth; let stand until liquid is absorbed, stirring occasionally. Stir in remaining ingredients, except tomatoes and lettuce. Without slicing all the way through, cut each tomato into 6 wedges; place on lettuce lined plates. Gently open tomatoes. Spoon pilaf into centers.

Rice Salad Ole' (6 servings)

1 Tbsp. peanut oil
1 cup raw brown rice
2½ cups vegetable stock
1 Tbsp. chili powder
2 tsp. cumin
½ tsp. sea salt
½ cup chopped red onion
1 clove garlic, crushed
1 ripe tomato, chopped
½ cup diced green pepper
3 Tbsp. sunflower seeds
1 cup cubed natural Cheddar cheese
½ cup Guacamolé Dressing (page 90)

In saucepan, brown rice in oil. Add stock to rice. Bring to boiling. Stir in chili powder, cumin and salt. Reduce heat, cover and simmer gently until liquid has been absorbed (approximately 55 minutes). Remove from heat. Cool. Chill.

Combine chilled rice with remaining ingredients. Serve on bed of watercress or loose leaf lettuce.

Russian Salad (4 servings)

1 cup diced cooked beets
1 cup cooked kidney beans
2 medium potatoes, cooked and diced
½ cup diced cucumber
1 cup sauerkraut, drained
1 cup cubed tofu
¼ cup Horseradish Herb Dressing (page 92)

Combine ingredients and toss gently. Serve at room temperature.

Spiced Rice Filled Melon (2 servings)

1 cantaloupe, halved and seeded
2 cups cooked brown rice
½ cup minced Spanish or Bermuda onion
1 carrot, grated
1 cup raisins
½ tsp. honey
¼ tsp. sea salt
1/8 tsp. ground cinnamon
Dash nutmeg
Dash cloves
½ cup yogurt

Remove flesh from cantaloupe, leaving shell in tact. Combine flesh with rice, onion, carrot and raisins. In separate bowl, combine honey and spices. Toss with cantaloupe and rice mixture. Spoon into shells. Chill.

Sprouted Wheat Salad (4 servings)

1 cup sprouted wheat
½ cup green onions, chopped
1 cup chopped celery
2 avocado, peeled and sliced
1 pkg. cream cheese, chilled and cubed
¼ cup minced parsley
Lettuce
Dressing

Combine wheat, onions and celery. Arrange on lettuce lined plate along with avocado slices. Sprinkle with creamed cheese and parsley. Serve with desired dressing.

Tabuli (2 servings)

> 1/2 cup bulgar wheat
> **Boiling water**
> 1/2 cup tomato, peeled and chopped
> 1/4 cup chopped parsley
> 1/4 cup chopped fresh mint leaves
> 1/4 cup chopped onion
> 1/4 cup olive oil
> 2 Tbsp. freshly squeezed lemon juice
> 1/2 tsp. vegetable salt
> **Dash of pepper**

Place cracked wheat in oven-proof bowl and pour boiling water over to cover. Let stand 2 to 2 1/2 hours. Drain well. Add tomatoes, parsley, mint and onion. Combine remaining ingredients in jar with tight fitting lid; shake well to mix. Pour over wheat mixture and toss lightly. Chill overnight to blend flavors. Good accompanied with fruit and cheese.

Tofu-Green Pepper Salad (4 servings)

> 3 cups crumbled tofu
> 1/2 cup finely grated carrot
> 1/2 cup minced celery
> 2/3 cup finely chopped pecans
> 1/2 cup minced onion
> 2 Tbsp. freshly squeezed lemon juice
> 1 tsp. dry mustard
> 2 Tbsp. fresh chopped basil
> 1 Tbsp. cider vinegar
> 4 green peppers
> 1 clove garlic, pressed
> 1/4 tsp. vegetable salt
> **Dash cayenne**

In bowl, combine tofu, carrot, celery, pecans and green onion. In separate bowl, combine remaining ingredients (except green peppers). Mix well. Pour over tofu mixture. Mix gently. Cover and chill overnight.

Cut thin slice from top of green peppers. Remove seeds. Fill green pepper shells with tofu salad.

Tropical Pasta Salad (4 servings)

> *2 cups cooked soy macaroni, chilled*
> *½ cup finely chopped celery*
> *2 Tbsp. freshly squeezed lemon juice*
> *1 cup diced firm ripe banana*
> *½ cup shredded coconut*
> *½ cup broken pecans*
> *½ medium papaya, diced*
> *½ Papaya Seed Dressing* (page 97)

Combine all ingredients and mix gently. Serve on bed of greens.

White Bean Salad (6 servings)

> *5 Tbsp. safflower oil*
> *5 Tbsp. cider vinegar*
> *2 Tbsp. honey*
> *5 Tbsp. tomato puree*
> *½ tsp. vegetable salt*
> *1 clove garlic, crushed*
> *2 tsp. grated onion*
> *½ tsp. crushed celery seed*
> *½ tsp. Tamari soy sauce*
> *½ cup chopped green pepper*
> *¼ cup chopped parsley*
> *2 green onions, chopped*
> *4 cups cooked white beans, chilled*

Combine first 9 ingredients and mix well.

In small bowl, combine green pepper, parsley, green onions and white beans. Mix well. Toss with dressing.

Zucchini Pasta Salad (4 servings)

3 small zucchini, sliced ½" thick
1 medium green pepper, cut in ½" chunks
2 cloves garlic, crushed
¼ cup olive oil
4 oz. whole wheat spaghetti, cooked and drained
1 cup steamed green peas
½ tsp. vegetable salt
1/8 tsp. crushed red pepper
¼ cup grated Parmesan cheese
3 Tbsp. minced parsley

Stir-fry zucchini, green pepper and garlic in oil. Add hot spaghetti, peas, salt and crushed pepper; toss to blend. Just before serving, toss with cheese and parsley. Good served with a spoonful of yogurt on top.

Chapter 5

Fruit Salads

Apple and Carrot Salad (3 to 4 servings)

1 large Granny Smith apple, seeded and grated
2 medium carrots, grated
1/4 cup lemon juice
1/2 tsp. honey
Dash sea salt
Lettuce leaves

Combine apple, carrots, juice, honey and salt. Chill. Serve on lettuce leaves.

Avocado with Garlic Salsa (6 servings)

3 medium avocado
3 cloves garlic, crushed
1 Tbsp. crumbled basil leaves
1/4 tsp. vegetable salt
3 Tbsp. grated Parmesan cheese
1/2 cup olive oil
2 Tbsp. cider vinegar

Combine all ingredients, except avocado, and chill. Halve avocado and fill halves with salsa.

Avocado-Grapefruit Salad (6 servings)

3 avocado, peeled and sliced
3 cups fresh grapefruit sections
Loose leaf lettuce
Grapefruit-Honey Dressing (page 90)

Arrange avocado and grapefruit on lettuce. Serve with dressing.

Avocado and Persimmon Salad (6 servings)

2 large grapefruit, halved and segments removed
4 avocado, peeled and sliced
4 persimmons, quartered
Romaine lettuce
Yogurt Lime Dressing (page 100)
½ cup chopped raw cashews

On lettuce lined plates, arrange avocado, persimmons and grapefruit. Add desired amount of dressing; sprinkle with cashews.

Banana-Nut Salad (6 servings)

6 bananas, sliced
3 Tbsp. fresh mint, chopped
¾ cup chopped dates
½ cup chopped peanuts
Curry-Yogurt Dressing (page 88)

Carefully combine banana, mint, dates and peanuts. Add desired amount of dressing. Stir to mix.

California Fruit Salad (serves 6)

2 grapefruit, peeled and sectioned
3 oranges, peeled and sectioned
3 peaches, peeled, pitted and sliced
2 cups seedless grapes
1 cup cubed fresh pineapple
1 cup diced honeydew
½ cup Mayonnaise (page 83)
2 Tbsp. freshly squeezed orange juice
1 tsp. freshly squeezed lemon juice
1 tsp. honey
½ cup yogurt

Mix fruit together in chilled bowl. Combine mayonnaise with juice, honey and yogurt. Blend dressing with fruit just before serving.

Cantaloupe and Cherry Salad (6 servings)

3 cantaloupe, chilled
2 cups fresh cherries, pitted
1 head lettuce
½ cup Yogurt-Lime Dressing (page 100)

Pare cantaloupes and cut crosswise into thin slices; cut each slice in half. Tear lettuce into pieces and place in salad bowl. Dribble small amount of dressing over lettuce and toss. Add fruit and toss lightly with remaining dressing.

Cinnamon Apple Salad (6 servings)

6 firm, tart apples (Granny Smiths are great!)
4 cups water
1 cup honey
Dash sea salt
7 sticks cinnamon
1 cup natural Cheddar cheese (shredded)
⅓ cup Mayonnaise (page 83)
Dash Tamari soy sauce
¼ cup chopped green pepper
Lettuce leaves

Core apples; set aside.

In saucepan combine water, honey, salt and cinnamon. Bring to boiling, add apples, reduce heat and cook apples slowly, until tender. Drain. Chill apples.

Combine cheese, Mayonnaise, soy sauce and green pepper. Stuff apples with cheese mixture. Serve on bed of lettuce leaves.

Citrus-Avocado Salad (4 servings)

1 head lettuce
1½ cups fresh grapefruit sections
1½ cups orange sections
2 avocado, peeled, pitted and sliced
½ cup Honey French Dressing (page 91) *or*
   Honey-Yogurt-Mint Dressing (page 92)

Break lettuce into bite-size pieces. Place in salad bowl along with citrus sections and avocado. Toss with dressing and serve at once.

Citrus-Cheese Salad (6 servings)

> *3 cups grapefruit sections*
> *2 cups orange sections*
> *Lettuce*
> *1 (3 oz.) pkg. cream cheese*
> *2 Tbsp. yogurt*
> *¼ cup Honey French Dressing* (page 91)

For each serving arrange fruit sections, petal fashion, on bed of lettuce on individual serving plates. Combine softened cream cheese with yogurt and whip until fluffy. Place a spoonful in center of each fruit salad. Serve with Honey French Dressing.

Cranberry Coleslaw (Serves 6)

> *½ cup sliced fresh cranberries*
> *2 Tbsp. honey*
> *2 tsp. celery seed*
> *½ cup Mayonnaise* (page 83)
> *6 cups finely shredded cabbage*
> *Vegetable salt to taste*

Combine all ingredients. Mix well. Chill at least 2 hours.

Cranberry-Orange Salad (8 servings)

> *1 lb. raw cranberries*
> *2 small oranges, unpeeled*
> *⅔ cup honey*
> *Lettuce*

Put cranberries and pieces of orange through a food chopper, using coarse blade. Stir in honey. Chill for several hours. Serve on crisp lettuce leaves.

Date and Carrot Salad (Serves 4)

½ cup chopped pitted dates
1 cup finely shredded raw carrots
½ cup finely chopped celery
¼ cup Mayonnaise (page 83)
½ cup chopped peanuts
Dash sea salt
Dash paprika
Lettuce

Combine all ingredients (except lettuce). Chill several hours. Serve on bed of crisp lettuce leaves.

Fall Fruit Salad (6 servings)

1 medium pineapple, peeled, cored and cut into 1" cubes
3 bananas, sliced
2 firm, ripe persimmons, thinly sliced
1 cup seedless grapes
4 kiwi fruit, peeled and sliced crosswise
½ cup pecans, chopped
Honey-Yogurt-Mint Dressing (page 92)

Gently mix together fruit and nuts. Chill. Pass the dressing.

Fiesta Fruit Salad (6 servings)

¾ cup pitted dark cherries
2 bananas, sliced
1 cup seedless grapes
1 cup cubed watermelon
1 cup cubed cantaloupe
½ cup broken pecans
3 Tbsp. freshly squeezed lemon juice
Watercress
Yogurt

Combine fruit and pecans. Drizzle with lemon juice. Chill. Serve on bed of watercress. Pass the yogurt.

Fresh Mango-Papaya Salad (6 servings)

3 ripe mangoes, diced
3 ripe papaya, diced
¼ cup shredded fresh coconut
¼ cup chopped almonds
⅓ cup Mayonnaise (page 83)
2 Tbsp. freshly squeezed lemon juice

Combine fruits and nuts. Chill. Blend Mayonnaise with lemon juice. Top salad with Mayonnaise dressing just before serving.

Fresh Peach-Brown Rice Salad (4 servings)

⅓ cup yogurt
2 Tbsp. honey
2 Tbsp. freshly squeezed lemon juice
¼ tsp. sea salt
2½ cups cooked brown rice
1 cup sliced fresh peaches
⅔ cup sliced celery
½ cup chopped pecans

Combine yogurt, honey, lemon juice and salt. Add rice, peaches, celery and pecans. Toss gently. Chill before serving.

Fruit-Filled Watermelon (serves 6 to 7)

½ lengthwise cut watermelon
½ cantaloupe, peeled and cubed
½ honeydew melon, peeled and cubed
1 cup seedless grapes
1½ cups strawberries, halved
½ pineapple, peeled and cubed

Scoop pulp from watermelon, discard seeds and cube pulp. Combine cubed melon with remaining ingredients and fill watermelon shell. Chill.

For a decorative touch, carve a zigzag pattern around the edge of the watermelon shell before filling.

Fruit Platter (serves 8)

1 honeydew melon
2 pears
4 peaches, halved and pitted
4 sliced fresh pineapple
8 small bunches of seedless grapes (approximately ½ lb.)
Yogurt-Fruit Dressing (page 100) *or*
Honey-Yogurt-Mint Dressing (page 92)

Peel and cut melon into wedges; core pears and cut into quarters; cut peaches into quarters and cut pineapple into wedges. Arrange fruit on an attractive platter. Serve dressing on the side.

Fruit Salad (4 servings)

4 cups mixed fresh diced fruit
½ cup sunflower seeds
½ cup raisins
¼ cup cottage cheese
1 Tbsp. wheat germ
3 Tbsp. yogurt
1 Tbsp. wheat germ oil
2 tsp. honey
1 tsp. freshly squeezed lemon juice

Mix together fruit, seeds and raisins in bowl. Combine remaining ingredients in separate bowl and beat until smooth. Pour over salad and serve at once.

Melon-Cherry Salad (4 servings)

½ large honeydew melon, peeled and cubed
1½ cups pitted dark sweet cherries
1 tsp. grated lime peel
2 Tbsp. freshly squeezed lime juice
3 Tbsp. safflower oil
Dash sea salt
Dash pepper
Salad greens

In bowl, combine melon and cherries.
In smaller bowl, combine lime peel, juice, oil, salt & pepper. Toss with fruit. Spoon onto greens and serve immediately.

Mixed Summer Fruit Salad (serves 6)

1 medium honeydew melon, peeled and cubed
1 small cantaloupe, peeled and cubed
2 cups raspberries or blackberries
3 cups seedless grapes
½ tsp. finely chopped mint
Honey-French Dressing (page 91)

Combine fruit and mint in chilled bowl. Toss gently. Add desired amount of dressing and carefully toss again.

Orange-Cauliflower Salad (serves 4)

2½ cups orange segments
2 cups raw cauliflowerettes
½ cup chopped green pepper
2½ cups torn spinach
⅓ cup Yogurt-French Dressing (page 100)

Toss Chilled ingredients. Serve at once.

Orange-Watercress Salad (serves 6)

6 oranges, peeled and sectioned
2 bunches watercress (torn into bite-size pieces)
½ cup Poppy Seed Dressing (page 97)

Toss oranges with watercress. Add dressing and toss to coat well.

Peach-Pecan Salad (4 servings)

3 cups diced peaches
1½ cups diced celery
1 cup chopped pecans
⅔ cup yogurt
2 tsp. honey
Lettuce leaves

Line bowl with lettuce leaves.
In separate bowl, combine celery, nuts, yogurt and honey. Mix well. Add peaches. Spoon onto lettuce.

Persimmon Salad (serves 4)

4 ripe persimmon, sliced
Romaine lettuce
¼ cup yogurt
1 tsp. freshly squeezed lime juice
½ cup chopped raw cashews

Arrange persimmon slices on bed of Romaine lettuce.
Combine yogurt with lime juice. Spoon over persimmon. Sprinkle cashews over top.

Persimmon Salad with Avocado (6 servings)

3 ripe persimmon, each cut into eighths
2 ripe avocado, peeled and cut into thick slices
2 grapefruit, peeled and sectioned
2 Tbsp. freshly squeezed lemon juice
Honey-Lemon Dressing (page 92)
Lettuce

Sprinkle avocado with lemon juice. Arrange persimmon, avocado and grapefruit on bed of lettuce. Top with Honey-Lemon Dressing.

Pineapple and Beet Salad (5 to 6 servings)

½ lb. sliced cooked beets
2 cups cubed fresh pineapple
Sections of 2 oranges
½ cup coarsely chopped peanuts
Yogurt-Lime Dressing (page 100) *or*
Honey-Lemon Dressing (page 92)

Mix beets with fruit and peanuts. Toss with desired amount of dressing.

Pineapple-Fruit Salad (6 servings)

1 medium-size pineapple
1 banana, sliced
2 ripe nectarines, sliced
Freshly squeezed lemon juice
1 cup sliced strawberries
1 cup honeydew, cubed
Ginger-Yogurt Dressing (page 89)

Cut pineapple in half lengthwise. Cut out fruit; cube. Combine cubed pineapple with remaining fruit and lemon juice. Spoon into pineapple shell. Chill. Serve with dressing on the side.

Pineapple Stuffed Tomatoes (6 servings)

6 ripe tomatoes
1½ cups shredded fresh pineapple
½ cup chopped almonds
2 Tbsp. Honey-Yogurt-Mint Dressing (page 92)
¼ tsp. vegetable salt
Lettuce

Cut slice from top of tomatoes and remove seeds and pulp. Chill tomatoes. Combine pulp with pineapple, almonds, dressing and salt. Fill tomatoes with mixture and serve on lettuce leaves.

Tossed Fruit Salad (8 servings)

1 head loose leaf lettuce, torn
½ head Romaine, torn
1 cup watercress, torn
4 plums, chopped
4 peaches, chopped
1 banana, sliced
⅓ cup freshly squeezed lemon juice
1 pint strawberries, sliced
1 cup green seedless grapes
Orange-Lime Dressing (page 96) **or**
Lemon-Yogurt Dressing (page 94)

Prepare ingredients just before serving. Toss to mix. Serve with dressing on the side.

Tropic Mango Salad (4 servings)

1 1/2 cups sliced fresh mango
1 1/2 cups sliced banana
1 cup sliced orange segments
Juice of 1 lime
2 Tbsp. honey
1/4 cup safflower oil
Loose leaf lettuce

Combine all ingredients except lettuce. Chill. Serve in lettuce lined bowls.

Waldorf Salad (4 to 5 servings)

2 cups diced apples
2 oranges, peeled and diced
2 bananas, peeled and sliced
1 cup diced celery
1/2 cup raw cashews or sunflower seeds
3/4 cup Mayonnaise (page 83)

Combine all ingredients and toss well. Chill. Serve on lettuce lined plates.

Chapter 6

Natural Dressing

Have you read any bottled dressing labels, lately? We're all busy, but are any of us THAT busy? Fresh natural dressings can be whipped up in a matter of minutes. Some of those garden or window-sill herbs you've been hoarding will compliment your fresh salads.

Speaking of complimenting, dressing should be used to enhance your salad, not destroy it. So be cautious when adding dressing. The most succulent salad can quickly be reduced to a soggy batch of leaves when its ingredients are forced to swim in the dressing.

Almond-Garlic Dressing

12 blanched almonds
2 cloves garlic
½ tsp. sea salt
¾ cup olive oil
¼ cup lemon juice

Put ingredients in blender container; liquefy. Chill. Shake well before serving.

Avocado Mayonnaise

1 ripe avocado, peeled and mashed
1 Tbsp. freshly squeezed lemon juice
¼ cup Mayonnaise (page 83)
¼ tsp. vegetable salt
1/8 tsp. pepper
½ tsp. chili powder
¼ tsp. cumin
1 small clove garlic, crushed
Dash cayenne

Beat together lemon juice and avocado until smooth. Add remaining ingredients. Chill.

Basic Blender Mayonnaise

1 egg
1 Tbsp. freshly squeezed lemon juice
¼ tsp. sea salt
½ tsp. dry mustard
¾ cup safflower oil   ½ olive oil extra virgin

Put egg, lemon juice, salt and mustard in blender. Blend a few seconds. Add 2 Tbsp. oil very slowly while blender is at lowest speed. Pour in the rest of the oil in a slow steady stream and blend a few seconds longer.

Basic French Dressing

1/2 tsp. dry mustard
1/2 tsp. sea salt
1/8 tsp. cayenne
1/2 tsp. paprika
1/2 tsp. honey
1 clove garlic, crushed
1/3 cup cider vinegar
1 Tbsp. freshly squeezed lemon juice
3/4 cup safflower oil

Mix dry ingredients and garlic together. Add vinegar and lemon juice. Stir oil into mixture. Shake well in jar or cruet just before serving.

Beet Dressing

1/4 cup cider vinegar
2 cooked beets, cubed (approximately 2/3 cups)
1 hard-cooked egg
1 tsp. honey
1/2 Tbsp. brewer's yeast
1 medium-size onion, sliced
1 tsp. fresh tarragon
Dash vegetable salt
3/4 cup safflower oil

Combine all ingredients, except oil, and blend thoroughly in blender. While blender is still running, slowly add oil. Blend until smooth.

Blender Green Mayonnaise

6 leaves spinach
1 Tbsp. fresh tarragon
1 Tbsp. Chopped chives
1½ tsp. fresh marjoram
1 Tbsp. fresh parsley
1 tsp. fresh chopped dill
1 egg
½ tsp. sea salt
½ tsp. honey
1 cup safflower oil
2 Tbsp. cider vinegar

Combine all ingredients, except oil and vinegar, in blender container; liquefy. Turn blender speed to low and slowly pour half the oil in thin stream over liquified ingredients. Add vinegar, then remaining oil in similar manor as before. Chill.

Caraway Mayonnaise

2 Tbsp. cider vinegar
2 Tbsp. grated onion
2 tsp. caraway seeds
1½ tsp. honey
¼ tsp. vegetable salt
Dash cayenne pepper
½ cup Mayonnaise (page 83)

Combine all ingredients and mix well. Chill.

Celery Seed Dressing (1 cup)

1/2 cup safflower oil
1/2 tsp. vegetable salt
1/4 cup cider vinegar
1/2 cup honey
1/2 tsp. celery seed

Combine all ingredients and mix well.

Cottage Cheese-Yogurt Dressing

1/2 cup cottage cheese
1/2 cup yogurt
1/2 tsp. sea salt
1/4 tsp. pepper
2 hard-cooked eggs, mashed
1 Tbsp. minced green pepper
1 Tbsp. minced onion
1 tsp. caraway seed

Blend ingredients in blender container until smooth. Chill.

Cranberry Dressing

2/3 cup fresh cranberries
2 Tbsp. apple juice
3 Tbsp. honey
1 Tbsp. lemon juice
1/3 cup yogurt
3 Tbsp. sunflower seed oil

Blend all ingredients until smooth. Great on fruit salads!

Creamy Avocado Dressing

1 cup mashed avocado
1 tsp. freshly squeezed lemon juice
1/2 tsp. vegetable salt
1 Tbsp. honey
1 tsp. onion juice
1 cup yogurt

Combine all ingredients and beat well. Chill. Good on fruit salad or greens.

Creole Salad Dressing

1 tsp. grated onion
1 cube vegetable bouillon, crushed
1/2 tsp. honey
1/4 tsp. vegetable salt
1/2 cup cider vinegar
1 1/2 cups safflower oil
1/3 cup tomato puree
1/2 tsp. Tamari soy souce
Dash cayenne

Combine all ingredients in jar and shake well.

Curry French Dressing

1/4 cup cider vinegar
1/2 tsp. vegetable salt
Dash cayenne
1/2 tsp. honey
1/4 tsp. paprika
1/2 tsp. dry mustard
1 cup olive oil
1 Tbsp. curry powder

Mix vinegar with seasoning and slowly add oil while beating.

Curry Yogurt Dressing

¼ tsp. sea salt
¼ tsp. paprika
Dash cayenne
1 Tbsp. honey
2 tsp. curry powder
2 Tbsp. freshly squeezed lemon juice
2 cups yogurt

Combine all ingredients and mix well. Chill. Good on fruit and raw vegetable salads.

Egg Vinaigrette

2 hard-cooked eggs, mashed
1 egg yolk
½ cup olive oil
1 tsp. minced parsley
1 tsp. minced oregano
1 tsp. minced chives
1½ tsp. minced thyme
2 Tbsp. freshly squeezed lemon juice
½ tsp. sea salt
¼ tsp. pepper

Mix hard cooked eggs with raw yolk. Add oil a teaspoonful at a time while beating vigorously. Add remaining ingredients and mix thoroughly.

French Mint Dressing

¼ *cup cider vinegar*
3 *Tbsp. minced fresh mint*
1 *cup olive oil*
1 *Tbsp. minced chives*
½ *tsp. sea salt*
¼ *tsp. pepper*

Mix all ingredients in jar and shake vigorously. Chill. Shake well before serving. (Tasty on either fruit or mixed green salads.)

Garlic Italian Dressing

1 *clove garlic, crushed*
1 *tsp. vegetable salt*
½ *tsp. freshly ground pepper*
1 *cup olive oil*
⅓ *cup cider vinegar*
2 *tsp. honey*

Mix all ingredients in jar and shake well. Chill. Shake well before using.

Ginger-Yogurt Dressing

1½ *Tbsp. grated orange peel*
1 *tsp. grated fresh ginger*
¾ *cup Mayonnaise* (page 83)
¾ *cup yogurt*
2 *Tbsp. honey*
1 *Tbsp. freshly squeezed lemon juice*

Combine ingredients and blend well. Chill. Shake before serving.

Guacamole Dressing

4 ripe avocado, pitted and peeled
2 Tbsp. freshly squeezed lemon juice
Dash hot pepper sauce
1 ripe tomato, chopped
1 cup yogurt
1/4 tsp. vegetable or sea salt
Dash pepper

Place all ingredients in blender and blend smooth. Serve over tossed salad.

Grapefruit-Honey Dressing

1/2 cup unsweetened grapefruit juice
1/4 cup honey
1 Tbsp. cider vinegar
1/2 tsp. vegetable salt
1/4 tsp. cardamon

Combine all ingredients and blend well. Chill.

Green Goddess Dressing

1 cup Mayonnaise (page 83)
1 cup yogurt
2 Tbsp. cider vinegar
1 tsp. fresh tarragon, chopped
1 Tbsp. freshly squeezed lemon juice
3 Tbsp. snipped chives
1 Tbsp. snipped parsley
1/2 tsp. vegetable salt
1/4 tsp. freshly ground pepper

Put in blender container and blend until smooth. Chill. Stir before serving.

Herbed Yogurt Dressing

1 1/2 cups yogurt
1/2 tsp. vegetable salt
1/4 tsp. pepper
1 tsp. dry mustard
1 tsp. curry powder
1/2 tsp. fresh basil, chopped
1/2 tsp. fresh oregano, chopped
1/2 tsp. fresh mint, chopped

Combine all ingredients; mix well. Chill. Stir before serving.

Honey French Dressing

1/2 tsp. sea salt
2 tsp. honey
1/4 tsp. dry mustard
1/4 tsp. curry powder
2 Tbsp. lemon juice (freshly squeezed)
2 Tbsp. grapefruit juice (freshly squeezed)
1/3 cup sesame oil
1/3 cup safflower oil

Combine all ingredients in blender container. Blend to mix. Chill. Shake before serving.

Honey Lemon Dressing

½ cup honey
½ tsp. sea salt
½ tsp. dry mustard
1 tsp. paprika
½ cup lemon juice
1 cup sunflower oil

Mix all ingredients, except oil, in blender container at low speed or beat at medium speed with hand mixer. Slowly add oil while mixing. Chill if not served immediately. Stir well before serving.

Honey-Yogurt-Mint Dressing

2 Tbsp. honey
1 cup yogurt
3 Tbsp. minced fresh mint
2 tsp. freshly squeezed lemon juice

Mix all ingredients together. Chill. (Perfect fruit salad dressing.)

Horseradish-Herb Dressing

¾ cup yogurt
2 tsp. cider vinegar
1 tsp. minced tarragon
1 Tbsp. grated horseradish root
1 tsp. honey
1/8 tsp. pepper
¼ tsp. sea salt
¼ tsp. paprika
1 tsp. minced parsley

Combine all ingredients and mix thoroughly. Chill. Shake or mix well before serving. (Good on tossed green or vegetable salads.)

Italian Dressing

1/2 *cup olive oil*
1/4 *cup cider vinegar*
2 *Tbsp. freshly squeezed lemon juice*
2 *Tbsp. grated onion*
1 *Tbsp. grated Parmesan cheese*
2 *cloves garlic, crushed*
1/2 *tsp. vegetable salt*
2 *tsp. minced fresh basil*
1 *tsp. minced fresh oregano*
1/2 *tsp. dry mustard*
1/2 *tsp. Tamari soy sauce*
1/2 *tsp. honey*
1/4 *dried red pepper, crushed*

Combine all ingredients in blender container and blend until smooth.

Lemony French Dressing

3 *Tbsp. freshly squeezed lemon juice*
1/2 *tsp. vegetable salt*
Dash cayenne pepper
1/4 *tsp. honey*
1/4 *tsp. dry mustard*
1/2 *cup safflower oil*   1/2 extra virgin olive oil

Combine all ingredients, except oil, and mix well. Then slowly add oil, a teaspoonful at a time, beating well after each addition.

93

Lemon-Mint Dressing

1/4 cup freshly squeezed lemon juice
1/4 cup safflower oil
1 1/2 tsp. chopped fresh mint
1/4 tsp. sea salt
1 clove garlic, crushed

Combine ingredients. Mix well. Chill. Shake before using.

Lemon-Yogurt Dressing

1 cup yogurt
2 tsp. freshly squeezed lemon juice
1 tsp. finely minced chives
1/2 tsp. sea salt
1/4 tsp. pepper
1/2 tsp. paprika
1/2 tsp. dry mustard

Combine all ingredients and mix until well blended. Chill.

Natural Cheddar Dressing

1 cup yogurt
1 cup grated natural Cheddar cheese
1/4 cup cider vinegar
1 1/2 tsp. caraway seeds

Place all ingredients in blender container and blend smooth.

Natural Mayonnaise

1 cup safflower oil
2 egg yolks
1/2 tsp. vegetable salt
2 tsp. cider vinegar
Dash cayenne pepper

In wooden bowl, beat egg yolks with wooden spoon until thick and creamy. Gradually, drop by drop, and 1/4 cup oil, stirring constantly. Add salt and 1/2 tsp. vinegar. Gradually stir in another 1/4 cup oil until mixture is thick and smooth; then add another 1/2 tsp. vinegar. Continue stirring constantly while you gradually add another 1/4 cup oil. Repeat procedure with remaining oil and vinegar. Add cayenne pepper. Store, refrigerated, up to 3 days.

Oil and Herb Dressing

1 cup safflower oil
6 Tbsp. cider vinegar
1/4 cup freshly squeezed lemon juice
1/2 tsp. vegetable salt
1 tsp. honey
1 tsp. chopped fresh basil leaves
2 cloves garlic, crushed

Combine all ingredients and beat well to blend.

Orange-Lime Dressing

¾ cup olive oil
2 Tbsp. cider vinegar
3 Tbsp. freshly squeezed lime juice
¼ cup freshly squeezed orange juice
1 Tbsp. honey
¼ tsp. sea salt
Dash paprika
3 Tbsp. chopped fresh mint

Combine all ingredients in jar with tight fitting lid; shake well. Chill. Shake well with each use.

Oriental Salad Dressing

2 Tbsp. rice wine vinegar
2 tsp. Tamari soy sauce
2 tsp. sesame oil
½ tsp. honey
¼ tsp. dry mustard
¼ tsp. vegetable salt
½ tsp. grated ginger root
2 tsp. toasted sesame seeds

Combine all ingredients in jar with tight fitting lid and shake well.

Papaya Seed Dressing

3/4 cup honey
1/2 tsp. sea salt
1 tsp. dry mustard
1 cup white wine or cider vinegar
1 cup safflower oil
1/2 cup chopped onion
3 Tbsp. fresh papaya seeds

Combine all ingredients, except papaya seeds, in blender container. Blend until ingredients are thoroughly mixed. Add seeds and blend to chop.

Poppy Seed Dressing

1/4 cup honey
1/2 tsp. dry mustard
1 tsp. sea salt
1/3 cup cider vinegar
2 tsp. onion juice
1 cup sunflower seed oil
3 Tbsp. poppy seeds

Combine honey, mustard, salt, vinegar and onion juice. Put in blender container and blend at low speed while you add oil in a slow steady stream. Stir in poppy seeds. (This is a traditional fruit salad recipe, but well worth a try on your tossed salads.)

Roquefort-Lemon Dressing

1/2 lb. Roquefort cheese, crumbled
1/2 cup olive oil
Dash cayenne pepper
Juice of 2 lemons

Mash cheese and olive oil together until smooth. Add cayenne and lemon juice. Stir well. (Great on tossed green or tomato salads.)

Seasoned Mayonnaise

1 cup Mayonnaise (page 83)
1 Tbsp. freshly squeezed lemon juice
½ tsp. chili powder
½ tsp. cumin
1 tsp. onion juice
¼ tsp. vegetable salt
Dash nutmeg

Mix together ingredients. Chill.

Sesame Seed Dressing

½ cup honey
¼ tsp. dry mustard
½ tsp. paprika
¼ tsp. sea salt
½ tsp. Tamari soy sauce
1 Tbsp. grated onion
1 cup peanut oil
½ cup cider vinegar
¼ cup toasted sesame seeds

Combine all ingredients in blender container and blend thoroughly at medium speed.
Shake well before serving.

Spiced Yogurt Dressing

1 cup yogurt
½ cup freshly squeezed orange juice
2 Tbsp. honey
¼ tsp. ground cinnamon
Dash ground nutmeg
1/8 tsp. ground ginger
1/8 tsp. grated vanilla bean
½ tsp. minced fresh mint

Combine all ingredients and blend well.

Spicy Italian Dressing

1½ tsp. dry mustard
1 tsp. celery seed
½ tsp. paprika
1 tsp. sea salt
½ tsp. freshly ground pepper (optional)
2 cloves garlic, crushed
⅓ cup cider vinegar
1 cup olive oil

Mix dry ingredients together; then add vinegar and olive oil. (Super on fresh vegetable salads!)

Vinaigrette Dressing

½ cup olive oil
1 clove garlic, crushed
1½ Tbsp. cider vinegar
2 Tbsp. finely shredded carrot
1½ Tbsp. finely minced parsley
1 Tbsp. minced chives
1 tsp. finely chopped tarragon
2 tsp. finely minced green pepper
¼ tsp. vegetable salt
½ tsp. dry mustard
¼ tsp. pepper

Combine all ingredients and mix well. Chill. Keeps up to 5 days.
Vinaigrette Dressing is excellent on vegetable salads or when used as a marinade for fresh sliced vegetables such as cucumbers, carrots or green peppers.

Yogurt-Lime Dressing

2 cups yogurt
2 Tbsp. honey
¼ tsp. vegetable salt
¼ tsp. grated lime peel
5 Tbsp. lime juice

Blend together all ingredients and chill. Mix well before serving.

Yogurt-French Dressing

1/8 cup cider vinegar
½ tsp. vegetable salt
Dash pepper (optional)
½ tsp. honey
¼ tsp. paprika
¼ tsp. dry mustard
½ cup olive oil
1 cup yogurt
1 clove garlic, crushed

Mix all ingredients together. Chill. (Good with mixed or fruit salads.)

Index

DRESSING

FRUIT SALADS

MAIN MEAL SALAD

MOLDED SALADS

TOSSED SALADS

VEGETABLE SALAD